Politics and the New Humanism

Politics and the New Humanism

Walt Anderson

Goodyear Publishing Company, Inc.
Pacific Palisades, California

Contents

Foreword

I have in the past avoided the traditional author's foreword, but this time I want to acknowledge some of the people who made meaningful contributions to my writing and thinking. Among them are . . .

Al Goodyear, who got me started writing texts, and Clay Stratton, also of the Goodyear works, who bought me a cup of coffee one day and opened a conversation that led, eventually, to this book.

Lew Yablonsky, who introduced me to psychodrama, at a time when I was just becoming interested in humanistic psychology, and thus insured that my development from then on would be not only a theoretical and literary pursuit but a fantastically rich and deep involvement with many people.

The people at USC—Fred Krinsky (now of Claremont Graduate School), Tom Greene, Bill Lammers, and especially Earl Carnes—who tolerated and in some cases even encouraged my interdisciplinary wanderings.

Floyd Matson, who recognized some of the basic political issues of psychology about twenty years ahead of most of us.

Fred and Mary Moore, with whom I have had so many really splendid arguments about all this.

Mike Murphy, of Esalen, and the other members of the group with which I was meeting and talking while working on this book—Joe Adams, John Vasconcellos, John Clancy, Stu Miller, and George Leonard.

A customary feature of this genre, I have noticed is a nod of recognition to the wife, usually for typing the manuscript and doing editorial work. I have a special debt to my wife, Mauriça. She got me started thinking about the "masculine by preference" business and about the irony in the fact that, in even the greatest works of humanism, the subject under discussion appears to be not men and women, but Man. I decided that in this book—except where quoting other authors —I would avoid talking about Man and talk instead about the human race or simply about people, and that I would use "he or she" instead of "he" when referring to an unidentified individual. It can be done, and it matters, and I want to thank Mauriça for that. She also typed the manuscript and did the editorial work.

W. A.

I. The New Humanism

What we really need, in trying to make sense of politics today, is a perspective. We have plenty of good theories, more data than even our machines can digest, and far too much method; we lack a fundamental sense of what it is all about, who we are, what we are trying to do and why.

We do have a perspective of sorts now—the set of procedures and assumptions called behavioral science—but it is a failure. Taking science to be a means of prediction and analysis, it failed to predict any of the political and social and cultural upheavals of the past decade, and it cannot analyze them either. It has failed not because science is a failure, but because this branch of science has drawn too many fences around what constitutes human behavior: it has excluded both the outer universe and the inner world of personal experience. We need a radically new perspective, radical in the sense of going to the root of things. We need a perspective from which we can look not only at politics but also at human behavior in the context of the physical universe, at contemporary events, and at ourselves.

It would help if we could give up, or at least modify, some of our ways of talking about political events and the ways we, as individuals, can relate to them. It does not do us much good to speculate about whether there might someday be a revolution in America; there is one going on, and the only thing which can prevent us from seeing it is attachment to a concept of revolution more appropriate to 1789 or 1917. Nor can we get far by agonizing about whether we should work inside or outside the system, because the system keeps changing all the time the debate goes on—and anyway there is really no inside or outside if we take a clear look at our evolving political culture. If we find a new perspective, look at political systems in terms of human evolution and at ourselves in terms of human growth, then perhaps we will be better able to understand the changes that are going on around us, and within us, and see new patterns of connection between the two.

Undoubtedly our willingness to consider a new perspective in the social sciences will be influenced by our opinion about how much social/cultural/political change is going on. If a great deal is happening, then it follows that some new ways of looking at events are called for; if we are merely going through a few rough spots, exaggerated by the media and the misfits, then perhaps we can all more or less hang in there and wait for things to settle down again. So I must make it clear, if I have not done so already, that I believe a great deal is going on. I think that the changes now under way in America and the world are probably more far-reaching and profound than even our most visionary writers proclaim them to be.

Obviously a change of this magnitude is not easily summarized in a phrase or two. But I think it would be useful at this point to begin to search for some kind of a conceptual handle. I have heard the term *cultural revolution* used frequently and have found it useful, but a more apt term, which one hears occasionally, is *consciousness revolution*—which means that all of us are undergoing a basic transformation of awareness, moving toward a different way of experiencing ourselves, our relation to history and to other people and to the world.

We can roughly compare this revolution to the Industrial Revolution, which was equally invisible in its early stages. We do not know precisely where or when the Industrial Revolution began, but we do know that it started, on a rather small scale, as a way people organized in relation to one another and to the production of goods. It was not basically mechanical; the machinery came later. Nor was it basically political, although everything political—and just about everything in the world— changed as a result of it. One specific consequence of the Industrial Revolution was its impact on political philosophy: it made it necessary for people who claimed to understand politics to pay attention to economics. This economic orientation is still with us, but it is no longer as valuable as it once was; the consciousness revolution will require political scientists to pay attention to psychology and biology.

In this book we will pay a good deal of attention to both of those fields, especially psychology. My main thesis will be that humanistic psychology—a relatively new intellectual movement, about ten years old now—offers us a perspective from which we can look at politics in general and especially at contemporary politics. Although humanistic psychology is fairly new as a movement, at least as an organized one, it belongs to an ancient philosophical tradition. And I think it would be helpful if, at the outset, we take a look at that tradition.

The Humanistic Tradition

Humanism has meant many different things at different times, and people of many different persuasions have called themselves, or been called, humanists. Plato and Aristotle are sometimes called humanists, although personally I am inclined to think that Plato's antagonists in the Sophist school—especially Protagoras with his assertion that "man is the measure of all things"—are closer to the humanistic tradition.

Greek and Roman philosophers are associated with humanism because they were rediscovered in the Renaissance era. Humanism was the essential spirit of the Renaissance, the philosophy and world-view of a time when human consciousness was breaking free from the doomed, sinful sense of life imposed upon it by medieval Christianity. A new vision of the world and the universe was emerging, augmented by the discoveries of scientists, explorers, and historians, and with it came a new vision of the possibilities of human self-realization. A historian of philosophy, Fuller, has described it this way:

The sudden and immense widening of the horizons of time and space set man thinking about himself. The book of human nature . . . had been opened, and therein he read with amazement and enthusiasm of the powers and opportunities with which nature had endowed him. The supernatural world retreated into the background. The pressure of heaven and the threat of hell paled in comparison with the prospect of the success or failure of his earthly career. This life was not a preface to life beyond the grave. It was a complete story in itself. It was to be seized, manipulated, exploited, refined, perfected to the full extent of the materials nature had laid before him and of his capacity for dealing with them. In short, human life as a natural event within a natural setting was not something to be died to daily; it was something to be *lived*.[1]

This humanistic spirit was fundamental to the voluptuous art of the Renaissance—which celebrated nature and the human body—and to the bawdy literature of the times, which found joy and humor in aspects of human behavior that had once been considered shameful. The Renaissance was an era when pleasure was taken seriously—Epicurus was another Greek philosopher who had been rediscovered, and was much admired—and it was a time when manners and morals, for all their shortcomings, were remarkably free of hypocrisy. And although the power of the church was waning, the times were not antireligious. Pico della Mirandola, one of the greatest of the Renaissance humanists, hoped to unite Christianity and philosophy with the old mystical religions, to discover some primeval human religious spirit basic to them all, and his concept of divine creation gave great freedom, potential and responsibility to human beings. Listen to his classic oration, *On the Dignity of Man*, in which he has God say to Adam:

I have given you, Adam, neither a fixed place, nor a particular aspect, nor any gift peculiar to yourself, in order that you may take your place and your likeness and your gifts through your own decision and choice. Other creatures are restrained within the limitations prescribed by my laws. But you, restrained by no such narrow bonds, according to the free will in whose power I have placed you, shall define your nature for yourself. I have placed you at the center of the world, so that from here you may survey all that is in it. I have made you neither heavenly nor earthly, neither mortal nor immortal, so that you, being your own free maker and artificer, may fashion yourself into whatever form you choose.[2]

Niccola Abbagnano in the *Encyclopedia of Philosophy* lists five identifying characteristics of Renaissance humanism: freedom, naturalism, historical perspective, religion, and science. Each of these is worth some brief amplification: by freedom was meant a general freedom to discover one's own potentialities, and a very specific political freedom against the rigid and confining structures of church, empire, and feudalism: "Humanism, which was born in the cities and the communes that had fought and were fighting for their autonomy and that saw in traditional hierarchical orders an obstacle, rather than an aid to the goods indispensable to man, defended man's freedom to project his life in the world in an autonomous way."[3] Humanism is identified with naturalism in the sense "that man is a part of nature—that nature is his realm, that the features which tie him to nature (his body, his needs, his sensations) are essential to him to the point that he cannot abstract from them or ignore them."[4]

The historical perspective—the rediscovery of antiquity, time, and change—is likened to the discovery of optical perspective in Renaissance art; it was a tool of consciousness, a way for individuals to widen their sense of the possibilities of life: "The significance of human personality as an original and autonomous center organizing the various aspects of life was conditioned by perspective in this sense."[5] Religion, even though it often took the form of opposition to the church, was a powerful force in the sense of personal life; one of the chief characteristics of religious humanism was tolerance. And science was seen, not as obscure, abstract and dehumanized knowledge, but as human, personal wisdom and power: "The conviction was affirmed that man is a natural being, that he is interested in making nature his domain and that he can question and understand nature with the tools that nature supplies to him, that is, with the senses."[6]

Some traces of the humanistic tradition were still alive in eighteenth-century Enlightenment thought, although it was being greatly modified by the new, mechanistic, view of the universe that resulted from Newtonian physics, and it was certainly a part of the strong sense of human freedom, the creed of the "rights of man," which came before the age of the great political revolutions. In the first half of this century, the chief inheritors of the humanistic tradition were the existentialists; consider the similarity between Pico della Mirandola's *Oration* and this statement from Jean-Paul Sartre's 1946 lecture, *Existentialism is a Humanism:*

When we think of God as the creator, we are thinking of him, most of the time, as a supernal artisan. Whatever doctrine we may be considering . . . we always imply that the will follows, more or less, from the understanding or at least accompanies it, so that when God creates he knows precisely what he is creating. Thus, the conception of man in the mind of God is comparable to that of the paper-knife in the mind of the artisan: God makes man according to a procedure and a conception, exactly as the artisan manufactures a paper-knife, following a definition and a formula. Thus each individual man is the realization of a certain conception which dwells in the divine understanding. . . .

Atheistic existentialism, of which I am a representative, declares . . . there is at least one being whose existence comes before its essence, a being which exists before it can be defined by any conception of it. That being is man or, as Heidigger has it, the human reality. What do we mean by saying that existence precedes essence? We mean that man first of all exists, encounters himself, surges up in the world—and defines himself afterwards. If man as the existentialist sees him is not definable, it is because to begin with he is nothing. He will not be anything until later, and then he will be what he makes of himself. Thus, there is no human nature, because there is no God to have a conception of it. Man simply is. Not that he is simply what he conceives himself to be, but he is what he wills, and as he conceives himself after already existing—as he wills to be after that leap towards existence. Man is nothing but what he makes of himself. That is the first principle of existentialism.[7]

Not all existentialism is atheistic, of course: one of the greatest of the existentialists was Kierkegaard, who talked of the human need for the "leap" into faith. But Kierkegaard resembled Sartre in his insistence that the human reality is indefinable—for Kierkegaard, this meant that the real existence of a person is always something more than can be conceptualized in any philosophical system.

And in some of the existentialists we get a different sense of the nature of oppression: the Renaissance humanists had been trying to break free of the medieval world-view and the strictures of Christian morality; the *philosophes* of the Enlightenment had fought against the decadent social order and the absolutism of unenlightened monarchs; for the existentialists, at least for some of them, the enemy was harder to personify. Indeed, that was the problem. Martin Buber wrote:

> The state is no longer led: the stokers pile up coal, but the leaders merely *seem* to rule the racing engines . . . the machinery of the economy is beginning to hum in an unwonted manner; the overseers give you a superior smile, but death lurks in their hearts. They tell you that they have adjusted the apparatus to modern conditions; but you notice that henceforth they can only adjust themselves to the apparatus.[8]

Buber, whom several major theorists of modern humanistic psychology cite as an important personal influence, worked with at least two ideas which will appear many times in this book: (1) dehumanization, the subordination of human meaning and needs to the needs of systems; (2) the existential encounter, the authentic meeting between individuals in which each recognizes the uniqueness of the other. Buber distinguished the I-It sphere, in which one experiences things—or people—as objects, from the I-You sphere, in which one enters into a *relationship.*

The idea of the encounter, as developed in the work of Buber, Sartre, and other existentialists, found its way into the therapeutic approach of the existential psychoanalysts. Members of this school, a forerunner of contemporary humanistic psychology, stressed the importance of an authentic human relationship between patient and therapist, and warned against the danger of attempting to reduce any patient's being to a mere set of intellectual descriptions. Relevant to this stress on authenticity was the conviction that the patient's greatest need was to make sense of his or her existence, to find a workable personal meaning. The search for meaning in one's own life, according to Victor Frankl, is a primary human motivational force, not explainable as the Freudians would have it in terms of simpler instinctual drives. And an individual person's search for meaning can never be taken over by someone else.[9] Another important influence on existential psychoanalysis was phenomenology; its concern with phenomena as they present themselves to the individual human consciousness was, for therapists, an encouragement to try to "get into" the world of the patient, rather than merely observe external behavior.

The search for a more meaningful kind of interpersonal relationship in the therapeutic process influenced the development in America of Carl Rogers' client-centered therapy, one of the major schools of humanistic psychology. This approach is one in which the counselor avoids giving advice or determining what the course and outcome of therapy must be, and shares that responsibility with the client. Rogers says:

> The primary point of importance here is the attitude held by the counselor toward the worth and significance of the individual. How do we look upon others? Do we see each person as having worth and dignity in his own right? . . . Do we respect his capacity and his right to self-direction, or do we basically believe that his life should best be guided by us?[10]

Underlying this approach is a view of human life—in fact of all organic life—as moving in the direction of "an increasing self-government, self-regulation, and autonomy, and away from heteronomous control, or control by external forces. This is true whether we are speaking of entirely unconscious organic processes, such as the regulation of body heat, or such uniquely human and intellectual functions as the choice of life goals."[11] Thus the counselor or therapist must not be an omniscient authority figure but rather a guide and helper; the ability of the client to find his or her own way is trusted. "I have yet to find the individual," Rogers says, "who, when he examines his situation deeply, and feels that he perceives it clearly, deliberately chooses dependence, deliberately chooses to have the integrated direction of himself undertaken by another. When all the elements are clearly perceived, the balance seems invariably in the direction of the painful but ultimately rewarding path of self-actualization or growth."[12]

In this country existential psychology and humanistic psychology were, and to a lesser extent still are, interchangeable terms.[13] This is true even though some of the basic propositions of humanistic psychology differ from the ideas of the European existential philosophers. Abraham Maslow, for example, refused to accept Sartre's notion of the human individual as a *tabula rasa*, a nothing which must make of itself something; for Maslow it was important to recognize the biological basis of human existence, with all that implied in terms of inherent characteristics. But in spite of this difference the same essential concern for personal freedom and responsibility is still in Maslow's biologically based theory of human existence. And it is one of the main concerns of all the various theories and therapies which make up modern humanistic psychology.

Humanistic psychology is a coming together of a number of different psychological and philosophical schools. Maslow counted among the charter members of the new "third force" Rankians, Adlerians, Jungians, neo-Freudians, Gestaltists, and Rogerians—as well as Herbert Marcuse, J. L. Moreno, Thomas Szasz, and Norman O. Brown.[14]

Two organizations have helped humanistic psychology to shape its identity as an intellectual movement since the early 1960s: The Esalen Institute of California, prototype for all the "growth centers" which have sprung up across the country, was established in 1962; so was the Association for Humanistic Psychology (AHP), which is still the main academic and professional forum of the movement. Among the founding sponsors of the AHP were several psychologists whose work will be cited in this book—Kurt Goldstein, Sidney Jourard, A. H. Maslow, Rollo May, Carl Rogers—and a number of nonpsychologists including Lewis Mumford and David Riesman.

In the past decade the various strains of humanistic psychology have coalesced into an identifiable set of theories and propositions, a kind of intellectual life style. And although there is a good deal of consensus—which I emphasize in this book—there are also still sharp differences on many issues. Some years ago a meeting of some of the leading lights of humanistic psychology was held, and I am told that, during the debates which took place there, one of the gentlemen bit one of the others on the leg. So remember that there are disagreements, that we are dealing with a perspective and not a single official and agreed-upon set of ideas.

J. F. T. Bugental, another of the founders of the AHP, has described this perspective as a "humanistic ethic." This has the sound more of a set of personal precepts than of a scientific orientation, but I think it is still a good place to start in getting a sense of where humanistic psychology stands today. Bugental lists as the identifying points of the humanistic ethic: (1) centered responsibility for one's own life, (2) mutuality in relationships, (3) here-and-now perspective, (4) acceptance of nonhedonic emotions, (5) growth-oriented experiencing.

Let us take a closer look at these. By "centered responsibility" Bugental means "that each person is the most responsible agency in his own life. While certainly recognizing the influence of contingency, of social pressure, and of concern for others, the humanistic ethic insists that these do not displace the person from being the one who mediates all such influences and in large part determines how they will affect his being." By "mutuality" is meant something akin to Buber's "I and thou" concept: "The ideal for relationships between people is one of mutuality between persons each of whom is the subject of his own life and each of whom values and recognizes the subjecthood of the other." The "here-and-now perspective" has to do with the development of awareness, of a constant attention to what *is*: it does not counsel ignoring either the past or the future, but it insists that understanding and change must be centered on the present. The "acceptance of nonhedonic emotions" is related to this, in that it takes all feelings, including "negative experiences," as sources of knowledge and growth: "Such emotions as pain, conflict, grief, anger and guilt are parts of the human experience to be understood and even valued rather than to be suppressed and hidden." The idea of "growth-oriented experiencing" is rather difficult to communicate in a few words, but it has to do with an openness to personal change, and a sense of life as a never-fully-completed process of development of one's potentialities.[15]

All of the above have a good deal more relevance to political change and to the practice of the social sciences than may be readily apparent; Bugental is talking about the idea of psychotherapy as a source of social change, which is considerably different from the "adjustment" goal of more conservative schools of therapy, and he is also outlining some of the possible characteristics of a widespread cultural change he calls a "humanistic evolution." But to come closer to matters which connect more easily to our present concepts of the study of human behavior, I will turn to another paper of Bugental's in which he discusses the differences between the humanistic and the behaviorist orientation; the humanistic psychologist:

1. Disavows as inadequate and even misleading, descriptions of human functioning and experience based wholly or in large part on subhuman species.

2. Insists that meaning is more important than method in choosing problems for study, in designing and executing the studies, and in interpreting their results.

3. Gives primary concern to man's subjective experience and secondary concern to his actions, insisting that this primacy of the subjective is fundamental in any human endeavor. . . .

4. Sees a constant interaction between "science" and "application" such that each constantly contributes to the other and the attempt rigidly to separate them is recognized as handicapping to both.

5. Is concerned with the individual, the exceptional, and the unpredicted, rather than seeking only to study the regular, the universal, and the conforming. . . .

6. Seeks that which may expand or enrich man's experience and rejects the paralyzing perspective of nothing-but thinking.[16]

These guidelines are equally useful to the social scientist; they help to steer us away from the peculiar kind of dehumanization that has crept over so much of academic research, taking the life out of both the researcher and the object of research. They encourage us to try to make the work of social science a rich and meaningful experience in which we address ourselves without apology to the purpose of making human life better and allow us to be ourselves—not faceless, valueless scientists but ourselves—while we go about the search for knowledge and understanding. These guidelines are not merely created arbitrarily out of a vague sense of how things ought to be, but they follow naturally from a certain set of propositions about what a human being is.

I will be able to present some of those propositions in this book; I will not be able to prove them, although a considerable amount of the kind of empirical data we commonly take to be proof is available. But we should be able to get enough of a sense of this humanistic perspective to use it as a working hypothesis; this hypothesis is comparable to the stance assumed by Rogers and his colleagues in their new conception of the role of the therapist. Rogers said, "The counselor chooses to act consistently upon the hypothesis that the individual has a sufficient capacity to deal constructively with all those aspects of his life which can potentially come into conscious awareness. . . . The counselor acts upon the hypothesis in a specific and operational fashion, being always alert to note those experiences . . . which contradict the hypothesis as well as those which support it."[17]

So what I am proposing, to those who find the enterprise attractive, is that we adopt as a working hypothesis the image of the human potential which the third force psychologists offer us, and see where it takes us as students, scholars, citizens. It is a risk, of course, because we may be proved wrong, but I think it is a risk worth taking.

Notes

[1]B. A. G. Fuller, *A History of Philosophy*, rev. ed. (New York: Holt, Rinehart and Winston, 1949), p. 6.

[2]Quoted in Niccola Abbagnano, "Humanism," trans. Nino Langiulli, in *Encyclopedia of Philosophy*, ed. Paul Edwards (New York: The Macmillan Company, Copyright 1967), 4:70. (Revised by author.)

[3]*Ibid.*, p. 70.

[4]*Ibid.*, p. 70.

[5]*Ibid.*, p. 71.

[6]*Ibid.*, p. 72.

[7]Jean-Paul Sartre, "Existentialism is a Humanism," Reprinted by permission of the World Publishing Company from EXISTENTIALISM FROM DOSTOEVSKY TO SARTRE. Copyright © 1956 by The World Publishing Company.

[8]Martin Buber, *I and Thou*, translation by Walter Kaufman. Copyright © 1970 Charles Scribner's Sons. p. 97

[9]Victor Frankl, *Man's Search for Meaning: An Introduction to Logotherapy*, trans. Ilse Lasch (Boston: Beacon Press, 1962).

[10]Carl Rogers, *Client-Centered Therapy* (Boston: Houghton Mifflin, 1951), p. 20.

[11]*Ibid.*, p. 20.

[12]*Ibid.*, p. 20.

[13]For explorations of common themes, see Thomas C. Greening, ed., *Existential Humanistic Psychology* (Belmont, Calif.: Brooks/Cole, 1971); and Rollo May, ed., *Existential Psychology* (New York: Random House, 1961).

[14]From: *Toward a Psychology of Being* by Abraham Maslow, © 1968 by Litton Educational Publishing, Inc. Reprinted by permission of Van Nostrand Reinhold Company.

[15]J. F. T. Bugental, "The Humanistic Ethic—The Individual in Psychotherapy as a Societal Change Agent," *Journal of Humanistic Psychology*, Spring 1971. pp. 11–25.

[16]Bugental, "The Challenge that Is Man," in Bugental, (ed.) *Challenges of Humanistic Psychology* (New York: McGraw-Hill, 1967).

[17]*Client-Centered Therapy*, p.24.

II. Conservative Psychology: Adjustment To Society

Our mind, that precious instrument by whose means we maintain ourselves alive, is no peacefully self-contained unity. It is rather to be compared with a modern State in which a mob, eager for enjoyment and destruction, has to be held down forcibly by a prudent superior class.

—Sigmund Freud[1]

My aim in this book is to present humanistic or "third force" psychology as a perspective from which to consider political events and the way we study them in the social sciences. I do not think there is, or should be, anything remarkable about using a school of psychology as an approach to politics, because the distinctions among psychology, sociology, and political science do not make sense anywhere outside of a college catalog. A psychology operates from an idea of what a human being is, and any such idea inevitably generates propositions about what human societies are, what they should be, and how they can be studied. Any psychology, then, is also a political ideology and a scientific methodology. And so, before going further into humanistic psychology, I want to take a look at the politics of the two other main streams of psychological thought, the Freudian and the behaviorist. For each, I will discuss some aspects of the theory, the kinds of psychotherapy that have resulted from it, and its influence upon the social sciences.

We will begin with psychoanalysis. All of Freudian psychology is concerned with the interaction of conscious and unconscious forces. In most cases this interaction is stated in terms of conflict; one psychoanalyst has defined the subject matter of Freudian theory as simply "human behavior viewed as conflict."[2]

And although psychoanalysis as a system has great scope touching on many aspects of human life, it is at the same time a system stated entirely in psychological terms. It contains a theory of political order based on conceptions of *internal* forces. "What is unique about Freud's point of view," Paul Roazen writes, "is that he always talks about authority in inner terms, that he always strives to see the meaning authority has for the internal needs of men."[3]

Freud's theory—that political order is an expression of inner psychological conflict—derives from a view of evolution in which the primitive does not disappear with the emergence of the higher species, but lives on and coexists. "In the realm of the mind . . . what is primitive is commonly preserved alongside of the transformed version which has arisen from it."[4] In an elaborate simile Freud once likened the mind to a fanciful image of the city of Rome in which the structures of all the phases of its history could exist and be seen together.[5]

In Freud's conception of the mind the higher levels are those affected by civilization, while the lower represent the uncivilized "ineradicable animal nature"[6] which is largely unconscious, and which has drives that cannot be tolerated by the conscious mind and by society. These drives have to be repressed, and Freud called the concept of repression "the foundation-stone on which the whole structure of psychoanalysis rests."[7]

Repression is also the foundation stone of the Freudian theory of politics, although Freud did not mean conscious political repression as the term is now commonly used. Repression is the hidden source of conscious, deliberate interpersonal actions by authorities against individuals, but in the Freudian meaning it is an internal and unconscious process of holding back undesirable instinctual demands: *"The essence of repression lies simply in the function of rejecting and keeping something out of consciousness."*[8] Freud described the mechanics of this process in terms of the functions of id, ego, and superego.

For the primitive animal nature, "the oldest of the mental provinces or agencies," Freud used the term id; the id "contains everything that is inherited, that is present at birth, that is fixed in the constitution—above all, therefore, the instincts, which originate in the somatic organization. . . . "[9] It is powerful and chaotic—"a cauldron full of seething excitations"[10]—and is also totally uncivilized, knowing "no judgments of value: no good and evil, no morality."[11] The id, furthermore, "has no direct relations with the external world and is accessible even to our own knowledge only through the medium of another agency of the mind. . . . "[12]

At a higher and later level of development, representing the organism's need to deal with external reality, the ego emerges. "The id is the older; the ego has developed out of it through the influence of the outer world as the bark develops around a tree."[13] Fundamentally the purpose of the ego is to serve the id, to assist it in meeting its needs, but since the ego is in contact with external reality it begins to assume an intermediary stance: "Its constructive function consists in interposing, between the demand made by an instinct and the action that satisfies it, an intellective activity which, after considering the present state of things and weighing up earlier experiences, endeavors by means of experimental actions to calculate the consequences of the proposed line of conflict."[14]

The third element in Freud's system—and the most important to his theory of politics—is the superego. The superego is the agent of civilization, "the successor and representative of the parents (and educators) who superintended the actions of the individual in his first years of life; it perpetuates their functions almost without a change."[15] Although the superego carries the values of society, of the external world, it is a component of the individual's *own* personality, drawing its strength from the antisocial aggressive impulses:

What means does civilization employ in order to inhibit the aggressiveness which opposes it, to make it harmless, to get rid of it, perhaps? . . . This we can study in the history of the development of the individual. . . . His aggressiveness is introjected, internalized; it is, in point of fact, sent back to where it came from—that is, it is directed towards his own ego. There it is taken over by a portion of the ego as super-ego, and which now, in the form of "conscience," is ready to put into action against the ego the same harsh aggressiveness that the ego would have liked to satisfy upon other, extraneous individuals. The tension between the harsh super-ego and the ego that is subjected to it, is called by us the sense of guilt; it expresses itself as a need for punishment. Civilization, therefore, obtains mastery over the individual's dangerous desire for aggression by weakening and disarming it and by setting up an agency within him to watch over it, like a garrison in a conquered city.[16]

As the superego embodies the internalized authority of society, it also performs the internal act of repression: "Since we have come to assume a special agency in the ego, the super-ego, which represents demands of a restrictive and rejecting character, we may say that repression is the work of this super-ego and that it is carried out either by itself or by the ego in obedience to its orders."[17]

In a historical sense we can see the emergence of Freudian theory as a recognition of the enormous demands placed upon the human instinctual system by the various forces of nineteenth- and twentieth-century Europe: Victorian morality, nationalism, the increasing bureaucratization and organization of life. Such demands, for Freud, were inherent in the process of civilization itself. "It is impossible," he wrote, "to overlook the extent to which civilization is built up upon a renunciation of instinct, how much it presupposes precisely the non-satisfaction . . . of powerful instincts."[18]

He did not believe that a life of gratification of those instincts offered any great promise. Research among primitive peoples, he said, showed that "their instinctual life is by no means to be envied for its freedom."[19] The situation of the civilized human being was one of having "exchanged a portion of his possibilities of happiness for a portion of security."[20] The task of the therapist was to facilitate this exchange, to aid the civilizing process by teaching people how to accommodate themselves to the demands of society, including those demands they had internalized. His only reply to a patient who wondered what value there could be in a therapy which made no basic change in the circumstances of life was that "much will be gained if we succeed in transforming your hysterical misery into common unhappiness."[21] Freud's lifework was in the service of the reality principle; Philip Rieff, who sees him as essentially a moralist, writes:

Therapy prepares a mixture of detachment and forbearance, a stoic rationality of the kind Epictetus preached. . . . To detach the individual from the most powerful lures in life, while teaching him how to pursue others less powerful and less damaging to the pursuer—these aims appear high enough in an age rightly suspicious of salvations. Freud had the tired wisdom of a universal healer for whom no disease can be wholly cured.[22]

In Freud's pessimism and resignation we find the source of his political conservatism. A radical philosophy, a revolutionary program, contains some concept of a possible better future, a resolution of the present misery; Freud's view of society contains no such concept. He has often been called a revolutionary because he discussed subjects which in his time were considered improper, or because he was critical of the morals and institutions of society. But even when Freud makes his case against religion it rests in part on the assertion that religion is a weak point in civilization's edifice of authority; he does not call for revolution, but hopes for a change that will *prevent* revolution:

Civilization runs a greater risk if we maintain our present attitude to religion than if we give it up. . . . Is there not a danger here that the hostility of . . . masses to civilization will throw itself against the weak spot that they have found in their task-mistress?[23]

Freud's rejection of revolution does not arise from an opinion about its desirability or undesirability, but rather from a conviction that true revolution is simply not possible; external authority is a manifestation of psychological need, an expression of the inner structure of the individual psyche, and therefore no real change can be effected by striking out against institutions. If social authority stands in opposition to some psychological drives—the more primitive ones—it also exists in fulfillment of other, quite powerful, human needs. Thus Roazen writes:

Patrick Henry's "Give me liberty or give me death" is, according to Freud, superlatively untrue to human experience. Man wants both liberty and restraint, and the tensions between conflicting needs comprise human tragedy. Freud's description of social restrictions, of the coercions of life, is so intensely real because he sees the extent to which outer authority is linked to our inner needs. Society is coercive precisely because its rules are internalized, are taken into the self; and at the same time society is useful in helping to keep some sort of a balance between various forces. Just as a child needs parental restrictions to handle his aggression, just as he needs to be stopped before the full horror of his murderous impulses becomes evident to him, so social restraints assist man in handling his aggression, both by providing vicarious forms of release, and by reinforcing his inner controls over drives which are alien to his inner security.[24]

In contrast to philosophies which view political authority as a result of a conscious and deliberate agreement among members of a society, as a necessary consequence of God's order on earth, or as a reflection of the economic system, Freud sees political authority as the external manifestation of an internal conflict. This internal conflict is largely unconscious and fundamentally unchangeable. The superego, the ultimate source of authority, is developed in part out of early childhood experience, in part out of deep racial memories of the conflict between father and brothers in the "primal horde";[25] it cannot be removed by social reformation. Freud's view of the possibility of human progress can be found in his gloomy prognosis that the sense of guilt "will perhaps reach heights that the individual finds hard to tolerate."[26]

Although Freud's system is based on a notion of evolution, it contains no prescription for future change, certainly no assertion that further progress is inevitable. Human development in his view seems to have reached a painful *detente* beyond which there is little hope of change. This view is a great contrast to that of Marx, whose system was also evolutionary (Marx dedicated *Das Kapital* to Charles Darwin) but who offered an inexorable dialectic of change and a utopian future of great freedom.

Freud offered no such promises, but instead worked to devise ways that individuals could learn to live with themselves and with civilization. He gave the world the first system of psychotherapy which contained as an integral part of its intellectual foundation a theory of society and authority. He was the first person who fully recognized the impact of modern society upon the human instincts, and he does not seem to have seriously considered the possibility that modern society could be transformed. He chose to become a teacher of ways of adjusting to things as they are.

Social Aspects of Psychoanalysis

The psychoanalytic profession as it has taken form in America is consistent with Freud's view of its social function, that is, it serves as a means of helping certain individuals adjust to the realities of modern civilization. It offers no program or rationale for fundamental political or social change.

In another respect, however, the psychoanalytic profession has evolved in a way far different from what Freud had hoped for. He wanted to see the benefits of psychoanalysis extended to a maximum number of people, and he hoped that analysis would not be exclusively practiced by medical doctors but also by lay analysts—"secular spiritual guides," he called them. But especially in America, psychoanalysis was taken over by the medical profession. So although Freud's ideas have had a wide impact upon the American culture, only a very small segment of the population has actually undergone psychoanalysis. It is thus quite limited in scope as a social movement; we have no idea what effects it might have had if practiced on a really wide scale.

The people who do undergo psychoanalysis are usually well-off economically. They have to be; psychoanalysis is expensive. Arnold Rogow, citing research already somewhat outdated in terms of cost, reported in his study of the psychiatric profession that "the average complete psychoanalysis totals between 700 and 800 hours at a cost of $25 to $35 per hour. Taking the lowest figures, a completed analysis will cost at least $17,500 over a period of three or four years."[27] A 1967 survey found that almost 99 percent of psychoanalytic patients were white, and that their education and income levels were far above the national average.[28] In contrast to other forms of psychotherapy, especially some of the behavior-therapy techniques discussed in the next chapter, analysis is paid for almost entirely out of private funds. Rogow's own survey of practicing analysts revealed that: "No analyst treats patients who receive public assistance or who are in Veterans Administration hospitals, and only one sees any patients in state or county hospitals."[29]

Psychotherapy patients also appear to come from a fairly narrow segment of the *political* spectrum. Rogow believes that "most patients, whether Republicans or Democrats, probably adhere to moderate or liberal political positions prior to entering therapy or analysis."[30] Few political extremists of any variety get into psychoanalysis, and when they do, according to Rogow, "the experience is not a successful one, with either the patient or the psychiatrist terminating therapy after only a few consultations. The major reason for the termination is the discomfort of the patient, or his doctor, or both, occasioned by the lack of personality rapport and the absence of shared values, whether therapeutic or other."[31]

There is no conclusive data on what, if any, *changes* in political persuasion are likely to result from psychoanalysis. Most analysts insist, no doubt correctly, that political subjects as such are seldom if ever discussed in analytic sessions. But Rogow's survey indicates that such change as does take place favors the political center: "The consensus of both psychiatrists and psychoanalysts is that successful psychotherapy, by promoting open-mindedness, relative freedom from intrapsychic conflicts, and a decrease in rigidity of belief, moves patients toward a moderate or middle-road political position if they were not already there at the commencement of treatment."[32] Any such change is likely to be minor, and part of a more general personality adjustment:

The patient's politics may be affected as he comes to understand the relationship between his life history and his political views and begins to ask himself why he believes as he does. To the extent that his political convictions are based more on the remote past than the present, or serve personality needs that change or disappear under therapy, these convictions are likely to undergo modification. The revision of political views, of course, need not be, and probably rarely is, dramatic, such as a shift from one party to another or from one ideology to its direct opposite. On the whole, it is doubtful that as a result of therapy or analysis, a patient would transfer his loyalties from, say, George Wallace to Eugene McCarthy, but it is conceivable that his allegiance might shift from Barry Goldwater or Ronald Reagan to Nelson Rockefeller. The effects, if any, are likely to find expression as a move *from more extreme positions to the moderate center* of American politics, whether in the Republican or Democratic party.[33]

This statement, if nothing else, reveals an implicit value assumption about politics and mental health: namely, that the more healthy individual occupies a "middle-of-the-road" political position. This assumption is consistent with a view of therapy as adjustment, and with the values which are to be found in applications of Freudian theory to political analysis.

Freudian Political Science

Although Freudian psychology has definitely had some impact upon political science, it has not been a major one. Roazen rates the influence as smaller than that upon other disciplines:

If one were to construct a spectrum of the social sciences on the basis of the attention that each discipline has paid to a psychoanalytic view of personality factors, the range would run from economics, where the impact of Freud would be close to zero, to cultural anthropology, where psychoanalysis has made its most notable contribution. Political science would fall toward the middle of the spectrum, but probably rather nearer to economics than to cultural anthropology.[34]

One of the first Americans to take serious note of the implications of Freudian theory for political science was Walter Lippmann, who used some of Freud's concepts in works published prior to 1930.[35] But Lippmann did not attempt to develop a Freudian theory of political behavior; that task was taken up in the 1930s by Harold Lasswell, a political scientist who had made a comprehensive study of Freud's writings and had undergone a training analysis.

In his *Psychopathology and Politics* Lasswell made extensive use of Freudian concepts and also of a "prolonged interview" method of research based on psychoanalytic technique. Although this work explored some new territory—including a preliminary formulation of political personality types—it remained faithful to the basic Freudian theory of politics as a manifestation of "internal" personality structure; it dealt with political behavior as a *displacement* of private motives onto political objects. Lasswell formulated the development of the political individual as follows:

The first component, *p*, stands for the private motives of the individual as they are nurtured and organized in relation to the family constellation and the early self. We shall have occasion to see that primitive psychological structures continue to function within the personality long after the epochs of infancy and childhood have been chronologically left behind. The prominence of hate in politics suggests that we may find that the most important private motive is a repressed and powerful hatred of authority, a hatred which has come to patrial expression and repression in relation to the father, at least in patrilineal society, where the male combines the function of biological progenitor and sociological father.

The second term, *d*, in such a formula describes the displacement of private motives from family objects to public objects. The repressed father-hatred may be turned against kings or capitalists, which are social objects playing a role before and within the community. Harmonious relations with the father of the family may actually depend upon the successful deflection of hatred from private to public objects.

The third symbol, r, signifies the rationalization of the displacement in terms of public interests. The merciless exploitation of the toolless proletariat by the capitalists may be the rational justification of the attitude taken up by the individual toward capitalism.

The most general formula which expresses the developmental facts about the fully developed political man reads thus:

$$p\}d\}r = P,$$

where p equals private motives; d equals displacement onto a public object; r equals rationalization in terms of public interest; P equals the political man, and equals transformed into.[36]

This formulation is an excellent statement of the Freudian theory of politics, and the basic dynamic it describes is present in later psychoanalytically oriented work by Lasswell and others. It asserts that political behavior is in some degree an acting out of internal psychological conflicts which are repressed, unconscious, and irrational; people rationalize—create rational motives for their actions but the motives they create are not the true sources of behavior

This formula naturally turns the attention of the political analyst toward the personal lives of political actors. Lasswell used a case-history approach in *Psychopathology*, and thus influenced the development of a new style of political biography in which the personality—in the Freudian meaning—was analyzed for clues to political acts. This case-study approach produced a new variation on the "great man" school of historical analysis, i.e., a study of the unconscious factors in the acts of leaders. Examples of such works are Arnold Rogow's biography of World War II Secretary of the Navy James Forrestal[37] and two biographies of Woodrow Wilson.[38] A logical next step from the study of the unconscious factors in the acts of leaders is the study of the unconscious factors influencing the work of political theorists; an example of the latter is William Blanchard's psychoanalytic biography of Jean-Jacques Rousseau, which examines Rousseau's revolutionary writings in the light of his sexual and aggressive drives and conflicts.[39]

Revolutionaries and revolutionary movements do not fare very well at the handhands of Freudian political analysts. The internal theory of authority as expressed through Lasswell's displacement formula tends inescapably toward a view of any action against constituted authorities as an acting out of repressed hostility. Such an emphasis makes it difficult for the revolutionary to be taken seriously; his or her complaints against the power structure, however valid they may feel subjectively, are all too easily taken to be displacements: "The repressed father-hatred may be turned against kings or capitalists," says Lasswell.[40]

I believe that Lasswell, like Freud, considers true revolution to be ultimately impossible. In *Psychopathology* Lasswell refers to the short-run danger ("When the ruler falls, the unconscious triumphantly interprets this as a release from all constraint, and the individuals in the community who possess the least solidified personality structures are compulsively driven to acts of theft and violence")[41] and also suggests the long-run possibility of a return to authority in his reference to the "unconscious factors in the well-known tendency of certain political alternatives to succeed one another in crude pendulum fashion."[42]

In regard to Marxism, Lasswell also finds that the ultimate promise of the classless society is psychologically suspect:

The symbol of the "classless society" frees the omnipotence cravings of the individual to transform the world in ways most gratifying to his yearnings for power. The person is free to project his potency fantasies into the future, and to identify himself with this remodeled symbol. . . . Dialectical materialism is the reading of private preferences into universal history, the elevating of personal aspirations into cosmic necessities, the remodeling of the universe in the pattern of desire, the completion of the crippled self by incorporating the symbol of the triumphant whole.[43]

This antirevolutionary bias is one aspect of what I consider to be the inherent conservatism in Freudian political theory. This is not contradicted by the liberal political leanings of Freud himself, of most psychoanalysts, and of psychoanalytically oriented political scientists such as Lasswell.

There is nothing whatever in orthodox Freudian political theory to preclude a moderate-liberal political stance, favoring the gradual improvement of social and economic conditions. The Freudian conservatism comes out as a tendency to view everything *but* such a political stance as pathological, a failure of adjustment.

Thus *The Authoritarian Personality* gave us the F-scale, an empirical tool for measuring the kind of political deviance which was regarded as most threatening by moderate-liberals in the 1940s.[44] And in the 1950s, when fear of communism was at its highest, Lasswell and Rogow produced the C-scale, an empirical tool for measuring left-wing authoritarianism.[45] In both scales an extremely high score is taken as an indication of "pathological" authoritarianism; but we cannot overlook the fact that a high score also measures a degree of distance from the political center. And any tendency to equate political extremism with psychopathology carries the usually unstated corollary that psychologically well-adjusted people are likely to be found at the political middle-of-the-road. We will be able to see this conservatism more clearly when we look at opposing psychological systems which claim that political radicalism is an expression of the highest order of personality, and find the political center peopled with psychologically stunted individuals.

The Freudian Radicals

Orthodox Freudian theory and the psychotherapy and political analysis derived from it do tend to be politically conservative. But there have been persistent efforts—dating back to the early years of the psychoanalytic movement—to take Freud's insights and run with them in the opposite direction: to make the doctrine of repression the starting point for a program of political revolution and a transformation of human life.

The first of the Freudian revolutionaries was Wilhelm Reich, who in his stormy career managed to be expelled from both the International Psychoanalytic Association and the Communist Party; his troubles within the Freudian and Marxist movements stemmed from his attempts to tie the two together, an attempt which was unwelcome to the orthodox of both camps.

In 1929 Reich published a paper entitled *Dialectical Materialism and Psychoanalysis* in which he argued that psychoanalysis was a materialistic science, based on a description of conflict within the individual and society. Psychoanalysis, he said, was furthermore a revolutionary science. It located the source of sexual repression in bourgeois morality and thereby stated the case for a liberation of human instincts; at the same time, Reich granted that the movement seemed to be losing its sense of mission, and was degenerating into a business and a stylish fad.[46] Later Reich criticized Freud himself for placing his science "at the disposal of a conservative ideology."[47]

In spite of growing disillusionment with the main stream of the psychoanalytic movement, Reich continued to hold to certain essentials of Freudian theory, including the Freudian view of the *internal* basis of political authority.

Reich's most important book, *The Mass Psychology of Fascism*, was an attempt to explain to German Marxists why the economic crisis of 1929–1933 did not produce a massive conversion to Communism but, instead, the triumph of fascism. It was also an attempt to revise Marxism by adding to it a Freudian concept of psychological repression.

Reich believed that Marxism—especially the official version of it, the "vulgar Marxism" which was dogma for party leaders—did not sufficiently comprehend the condition of the European masses. Marxists understood *political* repression and economic exploitation, but these concepts did not adequately explain the situation. For some reason the masses were incapable of acting according to the political and economic logic of their condition. Instead of becoming revolutionary, they had a tendency to become reactionary.

So it became necessary to understand character as the basis of politics, to replace the idea of social classes in conflict with one of the character types in conflict:

Marxist sociology, out of its ignorance of mass psychology, contrasted the "bourgeois" with the "proletarian." This is erroneous. A certain character structure is not limited to the capitalist, but pervades the working people in all professions. There are revolutionary capitalists and revolutionary workers. *There are no characterological class distinctions in the biophysical depth of human structure.* The fascist pestilence makes it clear that the economistic concepts of "bourgeoisie" and "proletariat" have to be replaced by the characterological concepts of *"reactionary"* and *"revolutionary."*[48]

And while the economic forces in Europe were indeed such as might create revolutionary characters, the forces of psychological repression were creating a vast number of reactionary characters. Basically this repression was being done in the family, in the first four or five years of the lives of individuals. Reich explained the mechanics of it in terms quite similar to Freud's theory of the internalization of authority; in Reich's explanation, great importance was attached to sexual suppression:

> The moral inhibition of the child's natural sexuality, the last stage of which is the severe impairment of the child's *genital* sexuality, makes the child afraid, shy, fearful of authority, obedient, "good," and "docile" in the authoritarian sense of the words. It has a crippling effect on man's rebellious forces because every vital life-impulse is now burdened with severe fear; and since sex is a forbidden subject, thought in general and man's critical faculty also become inhibited. In short, morality's aim is to produce acquiescent subjects who, despite distress and humiliation, are adjusted to the authoritarian order. Thus, the family is the authoritarian state in miniature, to which the child must learn to adapt himself as a preparation for the general social adjustment required of him later. *Man's authoritarian structure—this must be clearly established—is basically produced by the embedding of sexual inhibitions and fear in the living substance of sexual impulses.*[49]

Reich saw the individual as caught by a kind of inner dialectic of forces, pushed in different directions by two different kinds of suppression:

> The suppression of one's primitive material needs compasses a different result than the suppression of one's sexual needs. The former incites to rebellion, whereas the latter—inasmuch as it causes sexual needs to be repressed, withdraws them from consciousness and anchors itself as a moral defense— prevents rebellion against *both* forms of suppression. Indeed, the inhibition of rebellion itself is unconscious. In the consciousness of the average nonpolitical man there is not even a trace of it.[50]

The interference with normal sexuality in the authoritarian family, then, was what maintained the authoritarian state. This is why "the authoritarian state gains an enormous interest in the authoritarian family: *It becomes the factory in which the state's structure and ideology are molded.*"[51] And it is also the key to understanding the great flaw in the conventional, economically deterministic Marxist ideology: *"Sexual inhibition alters the structure of the economically suppressed individual in such a manner that he thinks, feels and acts against his own material interests."*[52]

We have seen that the theory of internalized authority as it was originally stated by Freud led logically to a pessimistic attitude toward social change; this is true of Reich as well. Reich *did* believe that revolution was possible—and he believed passionately that it was necessary—but he was skeptical about "instant revolution," overnight change by winning control of political institutions. True revolution would have to go on for a generation or more, change all interpersonal arrangements, raise a generation of enlightened children, and clean out the "conservative infestation of the workers."[53]

Although Reich always suffered from a certain lack of respectability he influenced many other psychologists and political thinkers, and his ideas are still with us in many ways. They can be found in the work of the gestalt therapists, in a number of body-oriented approaches to therapy (such as bioenergetics), and in new attempts to understand politics in psychological rather than socioeconomic terms.

Since Reich's time there have been other reinterpreters of Freud, most notably Herbert Marcuse and Norman O. Brown. Each of these has found in Freudian theory a promise of human liberation, and both have attained great popular status as the philosophical mentors of rebellious youth. According to Theodore Roszak: "The emergence of Herbert Marcuse and Norman Brown as major social theorists among the disaffiliated young of Western Europe and America must be taken as one of the defining features of the counter culture."[54]

Reich, Marcuse, and Brown agree on seeing the description of the repressive nature of life in modern society as something that must be changed. They all have different programs for bringing the change about: Reich believed in the liberative possibilities of psychotherapy; Marcuse holds out for political revolution; Brown envisions a human renaissance transcending politics itself. But the agreement is more important than the difference: it boils down to a belief that people are capable of being free. And that adjustment to unfreedom is not the same thing as mental health. The approach to political analysis that flows from this perspective is quite different from that of the orthodox Freudians. Reich sums it up succinctly: "What is to be explained," he said, "is not why the starving individual steals or why the exploited individual strikes, but why the majority of starving individuals do *not* steal and the majority of exploited individuals do *not* strike.[55]

Notes—

[1]Sigmund Freud, "My Contact with Josef Popper-Lynkeus," (1932) trans. James Strachey, in *Character and Culture* from Collier Books edition of *The Collected Papers of Sigmund Freud* (New York: Crowell-Collier, 1963), p. 303.

[2]Reprinted from *Freedom and Experience: Essays Presented to Horace M. Kallen*, edited by Sidney Hook and Milton R. Konvitz. Copyright 1947 by Cornell University Press. Used with permission of Cornell University Press. p. 241.

[3]Paul Roazen, *Freud: Political and Social Thought* (New York: Knopf, 1968), p. 157.

[4]Sigmund Freud, *Civilization and Its Discontents* (1930), trans. James Strachey (New York: W. W. Norton, 1951), p. 15. Also in volume XXI of *The Standard Edition of the Complete Psychological Works of Sigmund Freud*. (London: The Hogarth Press).

[5]*Ibid.*, p. 17.

[6]Freud, *A General Introduction to Psychoanalysis* (1916–17), trans. G. Stanley Hall (New York: Boni and Liveright, 1920), p. 247.

[7]Freud, "On the History of the Psychoanalytic Movement" (1914), trans. Joan Riviere in *The History of the Psychoanalytic Movement* from Collier Books edition of *The Collected Papers of Sigmund Freud* (New York: Crowell-Collier, 1963), p. 50.

[8]Freud, "Repression" (1915), trans. Cecil M. Baines in *General Psychological Theory* from Collier Books edition of *The Collected Papers of Sigmund Freud* (New York: Crowell-Collier, 1963), p. 105.

[9]Freud, *An Outline of Psychoanalysis* (1940), trans. James Strachey (New York: W. W. Norton, 1949), p. 14.

[10]Freud, *New Introductory Lectures on Psychoanalysis* (1933), trans. James Strachey (New York: W. W. Norton, 1965), p. 73.

[11] *Ibid.*, p. 74.

[12] *An Outline of Psychoanalysis*, p. 108.

[13] Freud, *Moses and Monotheism*, trans. Katherine Jones (New York: Alfred A. Knopf, Inc., © 1939), p. 152.

[14] *An Outline of Psychoanalysis*, p. 110.

[15] *Moses and Monotheism*, p. 184.

[16] *Civilization and Its Discontents*, pp. 70–71.

[17] *New Introductory Lectures on Psychoanalysis*, p. 69.

[18] *Civilization and Its Discontents*, p. 44.

[19] *Ibid.*, p. 62.

[20] *Ibid.*

[21] Freud, with Josef Breuer, *Studies on Hysteria* (1893), trans. James Strachey (London: Hogarth Press, 1955), p. 305.

[22] Philip Rieff, *Freud: The Mind of the Moralist* (New York: Viking Press, 1959), p. 327.

[23] Freud, *The Future of an Illusion*, trans. James Strachey (London: Hogarth Press, 1961), p. 39.

[24] Roazen, *Freud.*, pp. 157–158.

[25] *Civilization and Its Discontents*, pp. 78–79.

[26] *Ibid.*, p. 80.

[27] Reprinted by permission of G. P. Putnam's Sons from *The Psychiatrists* by Arnold Rogow. Copyright © 1970 by Arnold Rogow. p. 24.

[28] *Ibid.*, p. 81.

[29] *Ibid.*, p. 62.

[30] *Ibid.*, p. 145.

[31] *Ibid.*, p. 75.

[32] *Ibid.*, p. 72.

[33] *Ibid.*, pp. 145–146. Italics added.

[34] Roazen, *Freud*, p. 37.

[35] Walter Lippmann, *A Preface to Politics* (New York: Mitchell Kennedy, 1913); and *Public Opinion* (New York: Harcourt, Brace & World, 1922).

[36] Harold D. Lasswell, *Psychopathology and Politics* (Chicago: University of Chicago Press, 1930), pp. 74–76.

[37] Arnold Rogow, *James Forrestal: A Study of Personality, Politics and Policy* (New York: Macmillan, 1963).

[38] Alexander L. George and Juliette George, *Woodrow Wilson and Colonel House: A Personality Study* (New York: Dover Publications, 1964); Sigmund Freud and William Bullitt, *Thomas Woodrow Wilson: A Psychological Study* (New York: Houghton Mifflin, 1967.) The extent of Freud's actual participation in the latter is in doubt.

[39] William H. Blanchard, *Rousseau and the Spirit of Revolution: A Psychological Study* (Ann Arbor: University of Michigan Press, 1967.)

[40] *Psychopathology and Politics*, pp. 74–76.

[41] *Psychopathology and Politics*, p. 180.

[42] *Ibid.*, p. 181.

[43] Lasswell, "The Strategy of Revolutionary and War Propaganda," in *Public Opinion and World Politics* ed. Quincy Wright (Chicago: University of Chicago Press, 1933), pp. 207–209.

[44] T. W. Adorno et al, *The Authoritarian Personality* (New York: Harper and Row, 1950).

[45] Rogow, *The Psychiatrists*, p. 241.

[46] Paul A. Robinson, *The Freudian Left* (New York: Harper Colophon Books, 1969), pp. 41–42.

[47] Wilhelm Reich, *The Function of the Orgasm* (New York: Noonday Press, 1942), p. 195.

[48] Reich, *The Mass Psychology of Fascism* (1933), trans. Theodore P. Wolfe (New York: Orgone Institute Press, 1946), pp. xx–xxi.

[49] Reich, *The Mass Psychology of Fascism* (New York: Farrar, Straus & Giroux, 1970), p. 30. (trans. Vincent R. Carfagno.)

[50] *Ibid.*, p. 31.

[51] *Ibid.*, p. 30.

[52]Reich, *The Mass Psychology of Fascism* (1933) translated by Theodore P. Wolfe (New York: Orgone Institute. Press, 1946) p. 26.
[53]*Ibid.*, p. 59. See also Rieff, *op. cit.* pp. 160–161.
[54]Theodore Roszak, *The Making of a Counter Culture* (New York: Doubleday Anchor, 1969). p. 84.
[55]*Mass Psychology of Fascism*, translated by Theodore P. Wolfe. p. 15.

III. Conservative Psychology: The Control of Behavior

The interest of the behaviorist is more than the interest of a spectator—he wants to control man's reactions as physical scientists want to control and manipulate other natural phenomena.

—J. B. Watson[1]

The behavioral movement in psychology was in part a protest against the rather murky concepts and methods of traditional psychology. Although it was getting under way at about the same time as the Freudian psychoanalytic movement it became in time a protest against Freud as well. Freud was an innovator in many ways, but one of his main sources of information was the time-honored technique of introspection. The first person he analyzed was himself, and he used his own dreams to generalize about the symbolism of dreaming itself; also his patients contributed to the development of his theories as they underwent therapy. Although Freud considered himself a scientist and has been accepted as such by some social scientists,[2] many others have felt that he employed unnecessary concepts and a methodology that made it impossible to either verify or disprove his theories.

Behaviorism is in large part an organized reaction to such concepts and methods. The behaviorists have insisted upon a psychological science comparable to other sciences; they have rejected introspection as a scientific method and have also rejected such concepts as mind and consciousness. J. B. Watson, the best-known early spokesman for the behaviorist movement in America, described the urge toward a more scientific psychology as follows:

[Psychologists] reached the conclusion that they could no longer be content to work with the *intangibles.* They saw their brother scientists making progress in medicine, in chemistry, in physics. Every new discovery in those fields was of prime importance, every new element isolated in one laboratory could be isolated in some other laboratory; each new element was immediately taken up in the warp and woof of science as a whole. . . . The behaviorist began his own formulation of the problem of psychology by sweeping aside all medieval subjective terms such as sensation, perception, image, desire, purpose, and even thinking and emotion as they were originally defined. . . . The behaviorist asks: why don't we make what we can observe the real field of psychology? Let us limit ourselves to things that can be observed and formulate laws concerning only the observable things.[3]

When Watson began to popularize behaviorism the movement had already produced a substantial body of theory and research. E. L. Thorndike in America had published studies on animal learning and had formulated his basic law of affect (that an animal will repeat actions which gain it satisfaction and avoid actions which cause it discomfort) which was fundamental to later behaviorist research.[4] Pavlov in Russia had won a Nobel Prize for his experiments with gastrointestinal secretions and was beginning to investigate the possibility that such bodily processes could be not simply inherited (unconditioned) reflexes but also acquired, *learned* responses to artificial stimuli.[5]

Behaviorism was congenial to the pragmatic, positivistic spirit of philosophy in America and to the popular interest in and respect for scientific progress. It became both a powerful academic influence, particularly in departments of psychology, and, mostly through Watson's efforts, a topic of wide popular discussion in the mass media.

Although behaviorist psychology was a complex and varied field of study, it had a number of identifiable common characteristics, among which I would include:

(1) avoidance of internal psychological constructs.
(2) emphasis on observation of external behavior.
(3) attempt to find laws of behavior.
(4) parsimony, reduction of behavior to simplest components; experimentation with lower species.
(5) the stimulus-response paradigm, later amplified by the operant-conditioning paradigm.
(6) emphasis on environmental over hereditary determinants of behavior.

Also, it soon became apparent that the behaviorist movement was to be not merely a science but also a technology: not only a search for understanding of human behavior but also the perfection of means for controlling it.

Watson had in mind a gradual transformation of society through behaviorist education, which he believed would eliminate the sources of conflict between individuals and society. The behaviorist, he said, "would like to develop his world of people from birth on, so that their speech and their bodily behavior could equally well be exhibited freely everywhere without running afoul of group standards."[6] The kind of reform Watson envisioned was a gradual alteration based on education.

B. F. Skinner, the current spokesman for the behaviorist movement, advocates a more complete and deliberate program of cultural design. Skinner was and is fundamentally an experimental psychologist, whose theory of behavior is based on laboratory work with pigeons and rats. "The only differences I expect to see revealed between the behavior of rat and man (aside from enormous differences of complexity) lie in the field of verbal behavior," he stated in his first book.[7] His main conceptual contribution to experimental psychology is operant behavior; the corresponding form of behavior control is operant conditioning.

Operant conditioning experimentation resembles stimulus-response work in that it manipulates the environment of an organism and seeks laws based on the organism's observed behavior. It differs in that, instead of devising stimuli which will cause the organism to *react* in a given way, it devises rewards or punishments for actions (operant behaviors) already performed. Thus by rewarding desired behavior—such as by providing a food pellet to a rat that presses a certain bar in its cage—the experimenter trains the subject.[8]

The operant-conditioning approach obviously includes both negative and positive forms of reinforcement, but Skinner claims to have found that positive reinforcement is the superior training technique. His social-engineering hero, Frazier, argues this superiority in the fictional *Walden Two*:

Now that we *know* how positive reinforcement works and why negative doesn't, we can be more deliberate, and hence more successful, in our cultural design. We can achieve a sort of control under which the controlled, though they are following a code much more scrupulously than was ever the case under the old system, nevertheless *feel free*. They are doing what they want to do, not what they are forced to do. That's the source of the tremendous power of positive reinforcement—there's no restraint and no revolt. By a careful cultural design, we control not the final behavior, but the *inclination* to behave—the motives, the desires, the wishes.[9]

Skinner's confidence in the application of operant-conditioning techniques to large-scale cultural design soon brought him into a confrontation with the traditional notion of human freedom. "A scientific conception of human behavior dictates one practice," he wrote, "a philosophy of personal freedom another."[10] The Skinnerian case against freedom boils down to two basic points: (1) It is antithetical to scientific analysis of behavior and scientific control. "We cannot expect to profit from applying the methods of science to human behavior if for some extraneous reason we refuse to admit that our subject matter can be controlled."[11] (2) It does not really exist anyway. "We all control, and we are all controlled. As human behavior is further analyzed, control will become more effective. Sooner or later the problem must be faced."[12]

Skinner's most recent book, *Beyond Freedom and Dignity*, reprises the argument for cultural design that was offered in fictional form in *Walden Two*. The newer book is a kind of technocratic manifesto: Skinner contends that the behavior sciences are now sufficiently advanced to be ready to offer humanity a "technology of behavior" which can design the social order according to schedules of reinforcement in such a way as to maximize the happiness of its citizens and solve rationally the major problems that currently confront the world.

He states clearly throughout the book that he is advocating social control, not merely psychological influence or subtle coercion, to create and maintain the social order. The control is justified because it would be mainly an application of positive reinforcement—that is, people would like it—and also because the experts would themselves be part of the system. "The principle of making the controller a member of the group he controls should apply to the designer of a culture."[13] In spite of this reassurance, the fact remains that what Skinner explicity advocates is a nationwide (if not worldwide) operant-conditioning program.

Since Skinner regards most of the language concerning values of human happiness as unscientific and cluttered with "mentalisms" he does not state at any great length what values might guide the scientist in his work of cultural design, although he does grant that "the designer of a new culture will always be culture-bound, since he will not be able to free himself entirely from the predispositions which have been engendered by the social environment in which he has lived."[14]

The Politics of Behaviorist Psychology

Although behaviorist psychologists such as Watson and Skinner have been quite willing to extend their theoretical formulations to large-scale architectonic propositions about cultural design, they have tended to avoid identification with existing ideologies and have maintained that their concepts are above or beyond traditional political issues.

This tendency has not discouraged the critics of behaviorism from drawing conclusions about its political content. For example Floyd Matson, in a fairly representative summary of the case, writes:

Whether human conduct is conditioned or unconditioned it remains, on the behaviorist account, wholly determinate and predictable; and, in either event, it is open to manipulation by reconditioning. . . . It seems extraordinary nowadays that such a doctrine could ever have been construed in any sense as democratic: its blindness to personal intention, its scorn of mind, its denial of any freedom of action or capacity for it, its tacit enlistment in the service of a kind of technocratic efficiency and regimentation—these characteristics of classical behaviorism appear rather to confirm the harsh judgment of Mannheim that it bears an unmistakable resemblance to facism.[15]

The judgment of Karl Mannheim to which Matson referred was based on a historical view of behaviorism as a response to the need of modern civilization for a more efficient principle of human organization; behaviorism, said Mannheim, "is a typical product of thought at that stage of mass society in which it is more important, from the practical point of view, to be able to calculate the average behavior of the mass than to understand the private motives of individuals or to transform the whole personality."[16] The denial of the existence of inner motives and meanings becomes a simple refusal to deal with individuals in such a fashion; "Behaviorism is interested in human beings only as part of the social machine, not as individuals but only as dependable links in a chain of action."[17]

Mannheim does not allege that behaviorism and fascism are synonymous. He sees the two as different responses to the same demand:

It is not that behaviorism is fascist, but rather that fascism in the political sphere is to a large extent behavioristic. Fascism plans and changes the political world at the level of behaviorism. This is demonstrated by the type of propaganda in the various countries and the way in which it is used neither to change nor to enlighten the populace, but rather to subordinate it and make it loyal. Fascism creates an apparatus of social coercion which integrates every possible kind of behavior or at least brings it into an external harmony by force.[18]

The concern of behaviorism with the needs of society, and the shift of emphasis away from subjectivity, from inner experience, must inevitably produce a *social* definition of mental health and pathology. This has indeed been the case, and such a definition is now close to being generally accepted in contemporary social science. For example, Talcott Parsons: "Health may be defined as the state of optimum capacity of an individual for the effective performance of the roles and tasks for which he has been socialized. It is thus defined with reference to the individual's participation in the social system."[19]

The evaluation of the political content of behaviorism most common among its critics (and some of its defenders) is that it is technocratic: that it tends toward an organized mass society controlled with impartial and objective efficiency by experts. Although most behaviorists writing on cultural design represent themselves as the very essence of progressive thought, many people find behaviorism conservative as well, that is, preoccupied with greater efficiency, not profound change; with order and smoothness at any cost.

Richard Sennett, a sociologist reviewing *Beyond Freedom and Dignity* for the *New York Times*, analyzed some of Skinner's specific proposals for social improvement and found his political stance to be neither fascistic nor technocratic, but simply, in a bland, middle-American kind of way, conservative:

[Skinner] indicates a few purposes to which he personally would like to see the techniques put.
First, behavior control appears to him a way to get people hard at work again in an age where indolence is rife. . . .
As a corollary to his belief in hard work, Skinner rails against the sexual and other sensual pleasures that he feels have become rampant today, and argues that such behavior needs to be redirected. . . .
Not surprisingly, Skinner also believes that the small group, the town, the village, the little neighborhood circle, is the scale at which behavior conditioning can operate morally. . . .
These beliefs should sound familiar. They are the articles of faith of Nixonian America, of the small-town businessman who feels life has degenerated, has gotten beyond his control, and who thinks things will get better when other people learn how to behave.[20]

There is, certainly, a tendency for statements of the possibilities of behaviorist psychology to reflect the existing values of society, and this gives behaviorism a certain middle-of-the-road bias. For all the differences in philosophy and methodology that exist between Freudian and behaviorist psychology, they are rather similar in their tendency to operate as defenders of the social and cultural status quo.

Behavior Therapy

In 1924 Watson predicted that within twenty years Freudian analysis would be relegated to a place about equal to that held by phrenology, and a new kind of analysis, based on behaviorist principles, would have taken its place. The analysis would be the equivalent of medical diagnosis, and the therapy would be a reconditioning of the patient. "New habits, verbal, manual and visceral, of such and such kinds, will be the prescriptions the psychopathologist will write."[21]

Behavior therapy follows behaviorist experimental psychology in its value of scientific precision, its emphasis upon external and observable actions of the organism, its distrust of abstract "internal" explanatory constructs, and its interest in techniques of control. All behavior therapy techniques are applications of some form of positive or negative reinforcement, reward or punishment. Behavior therapists as a whole are not in agreement with Skinner's belief in the superiority of positive reinforcement. "In general," one psychologist stated recently, "behaviorists have found punishment to be one of the fastest, most effective techniques available for helping people rid themselves of troublesome behaviors."[22]

Behavior therapy looks at neurotic actions as learned behavior, as distinguished from innate or instinctive behavior, and thus its techniques are ways of getting the subject to learn a new, more satisfactory form of behavior.[23] Furthermore, it concentrates exclusively upon the empirically observable forms of the neurosis and completely bypasses any conceptualization of unconscious causes: "Freudian theory regards neurotic symptoms as adaptive mechanisms which are evidence of repression; they are 'the visible upshot of unconscious causes.' Learning theory does not postulate any such 'unconscious' causes, but regards neurotic symptoms as simply learned habits; there is no neurosis underlying the symptom, but merely the symptom itself. *Get rid of the symptom . . . and you have eliminated the neurosis.*"[24]

The term *behavior therapy* now takes in a vast range of approaches and techniques. I will discuss two schools which appear to have the greatest political significance: aversion therapy and operant conditioning.

Aversion Therapy

As the name implies, this form of therapy aims to create in the subject an aversion to a specific form of behavior. Such aversion is conditioned by the use of some form of unpleasant stimulus, which is either applied at the time the undesired behavior is performed or paired with the cues that normally produce the undesired behavior. This form of therapy, one study reports, "has been employed mainly in the treatment of approach responses which can be disadvantageous to the individual and which usually also incur social disapproval. Alcoholism, drug addiction, homosexuality, transvestism and fetishism are the conditions most often treated with aversion techniques."[25]

Commonly used in aversion therapy are drugs which produce nausea and vomiting; electrical shock is usually referred to in psychiatric terminology as "faradic stimuli."[26] Thus, in a case of male homosexuality, the subject may be given an emetic and then, as the feeling of nausea increases, be shown slides of nude males; if the therapy is sucessful the subject comes to associate the nausea with the homosexual stimulus and his homosexual desires are lost or greatly diminished.[27]

Operant Conditioning

This form of therapy, like operant-conditioning experimentation in the laboratory, manipulates the environment of the subject with the aim of training new behaviors through the application of positive or negative reinforcements. It may be used for anything from moderate forms of neurotic or socially unadaptive behavior through the most severe psychotic symptoms; it may deal with conscious and voluntary behaviors or with behaviors over which the subject has no conscious control.

Operant-conditioning techniques are in wide use not only in individual psychotherapy but also in large-scale programs for the modification of the behavior of inmates in institutions. There are, for example, "token economy" programs, which are operant-conditioning arrangements at the institutional level: good behavior is rewarded with tokens which may be exchanged for desired objects.

In one token economy program, reinforcements included "rooms available for rent; selection of people to dine with; passes; a chance to speak to the ward physician, chaplain, or psychologist; opportunities for viewing television; candy; cigarettes; and other amenities of life."[28] Desired behaviors cited were "enacting the role of responsible people who are adept at self-grooming, keeping their living quarters clean, dressing neatly, keeping a job, and interacting with other people."[29]

Token economy programs mainly follow the Skinner principle—use of positive reinforcement—but some also have punishment procedures. One program with punishment contingencies operated as follows:

The behaviors selected for punishment were those which typically elicit some form of punishment in a community, such as fighting, lying, stealing, cheating, physical or verbal assault, temper tantrums or property damage. The punishment consisted of the withdrawal of positive reinforcement, that is, tokens. The punishing stimuli consisted of two verbal pronouncements, "time out" and "seclusion," both of which led to the loss of tokens or the opportunity to earn tokens. When a member of the staff says, "time out," the resident is charged four tokens and must sit on one side of the day room for three to five minutes until his behavior becomes appropriate. Seclusion is used for more serious disrupting behavior such as fights, serious property damage, or refusal to go to the time-out area. When "seclusion" is spoken the resident is charged fifteen tokens and taken to an empty, darkened room where he must stay until he has been quiet for thirty minutes. If the resident behaves well in seclusion, staying the minimum time, he is reinforced with five tokens on his return to the living quarters.[30]

The author of the article here cited notes the resemblance of token-economy programs to the "labor credit" system in *Walden Two* and suggests that the token-economy approach "may be compared to Utopian planning."[31] He concedes that institutional programs are so far rather less than utopian, especially since those who run them are not part of the program; but he expresses the hope that in time this situation will be rectified, although "it will not be easy for professional people to permit programs which take the control of behavior out of their hands and put it in the hands of the patients."[32]

At the present time, of course, these programs are simply behavior-modification systems imposed from above on institutional inmates. They are in wide use "with institutionalized adults, mentally retarded subjects, delinquents, adolescents, and emotionally disturbed children."[33] The fact that they are favorably mentioned in much of the current literature is strong indication that they will be adopted in more institutions in the future. Many school administrators are now interested in "behavior mod," as it is commonly known.

In essence such programs differ only in scope of application from other operant-conditioning techniques, and operant conditioning is merely one approach to behavior therapy. But such programs make it far easier to understand why such critics as Thomas Szasz charge that all of psychiatry is in fact a form of social control[34] and these programs tend to become focal points for the politicization of therapy.

The Issue of Control

Ronald Leifer argues that any psychiatrist "who attempts coercively to modify an individual's thought, feelings or behavior . . . serves the purposes of social control no less than do the policeman and the warden."[35] This issue becomes particularly meaningful in relation to behavior therapy; here, the therapist so clearly controls the patient's behavior, and the consent of the subject is so much in doubt.

It is common for behavior therapists to discuss their various techniques as remedial measures undertaken on behalf of, and upon the request of, the patient. For example, Donald M. Baer, in the article cited above, defends punishment as a technique for "helping people *rid themselves* of troublesome behaviors."[36] In reality, however, consent is a rather more elusive concept; this truth is recognized by Meyer and Chesser, practicing behavior therapists, in discussing the difficulty of deciding when aversion therapy techniques may be justified:

The *quality* of the consent must be taken into account, particularly if the patient is being influenced strongly by someone else such as the Courts, a prison governor, employer or family. The psychiatrist may have more difficulty in deciding whether aversion therapy or indeed any psychiatric treatment is justified if the patient is referred primarily at the instigation of someone other than the patient, and he is not convinced that the patient is himself suffering as a result of his deviant behavior and wants help in modifying it. In such cases there may well be differences of opinion as to whether psychiatric treatment, particularly aversion therapy, is justified.[37]

This problem is taking on a new relevance in contemporary American politics because it also has to do with "rehabilitation" programs in prisons. Increasingly, progressive penal systems, such as those in California and New York, make use of the indeterminate sentence which allows the "rehabilitated" prisoner to be released after a relatively short period; this system is another example of the problem of the personal consent of the patient in therapy. The modern prisoner, according to Jessica Mitford, is trapped between the guard and the psychologist: "The prisoner who refuses to submit to therapy will find himself labeled 'defiant,' 'hostile,' 'uncooperative,' and the classification committee will act accordingly by confining him in a maximum-security prison. . . . "[38]

The issue does not concern only behavior therapy, but for two reasons this therapeutic approach is most involved: (1) behavior techniques are most vulnerable to legal criticism as possible violations of civil rights or cruel and unusual punishment, and (2) the various behavior therapies are more widely used than are Freudian or humanistic approaches to rehabilitation. Behavior therapy has a significant body of theory on criminal behavior, [39] a flexibility of techniques which can easily be modified to deal with specific and visible problems, a greater willingness to guarantee "results," and a greater ability to accommodate to bureaucratic needs for accountability and efficiency.

Behavioral Political Science

Political scientists generally insist on separating behaviorism from behavioralism. I believe that the distinction is, on the whole, a correct one: behavioral political science has relatively little interest in the techniques of controlling the behavior of individuals, and political scientists are seldom tempted into such grand conceptualizations of their roles as Watson and Skinner.

Yet there is a vast area of shared values between behaviorist psychology and behavioral political science. These shared values can perhaps best be accounted for by the influence of behaviorist psychology—in the 1920s already a highly developed body of research buttressed by pragmatic and logical-positivist psychology and popularized, mostly by Watson, in the mass media. On the other hand behavioral political science, an approach which was admittedly eclectic, did not gain a comparable academic ascendancy until the post–World War II years. Yet it may be that both movements sprang from the same soil, as expressions of the prevailing cultural climate of an industrializing mass society with a high reverance for science. Bernard Crick has argued that the form political science has taken in this country is merely a manifestation of our culture, that there is a "special plausibility to American students of politics of the view that politics can be understood (and perhaps practiced) by 'the method of the natural science.' "[40]

Several years before Watson appeared on the scene one of the earliest forerunners of the behavioral movement in political science, Arthur F. Bentley, was expressing the same distrust of internal psychological constructs—"soul-stuff" and "mind-stuff" as he called them—that would appear in Watson's writings years later;[41] Bentley's argument for the need to "get our social life stated in terms of activity and of nothing else"[42] was precisely parallel to the choice that was being made in the laboratories by the behaviorist psychologists. His insistence that "it is impossible to attain scientific treatment of material that will not submit itself to measurement in some form"[43] cogently stated the case for the quantification of the discipline that eventually took place. All of this preceded the emergence of behaviorism as an intellectual movement, although in his later years Bentley took note of Watson's work and expressed a "wholehearted agreement" with him on several points, including the "rejection of all terms dealing with consciousness or mentality. . . . "[44]

By the time Charles Merriam and his colleagues began to sketch the outlines of a new—and more deliberately scientific—science of politics, it was impossible for any American academic to be unaware of behaviorism; Edwin Boring, one of the most eminent historians of psychology, wrote that, "for a while, in the 1920's, it seemed as if all America had gone behaviorist."[45]

By the mid-1930s a behaviorist school was well established in sociology—sufficiently so that its critics were already beginning to complain about quantification, emphasis on externals, dehumanization of contents and excessive concern with methodology. And the subjects dealt with were roughly the same as those that would be taken up by the first behavioralists in political science: public opinion and voting.[46]

In 1943 Clark Hull, a psychologist, one of the most prominent members of the American behaviorist school and a leading theoretician of the interdisciplinary study group at the Yale Institute of Human Relations, published his *Principles of Behavior*. Whether or not it included as Matson suggests,[47] the first use of the term "behavioral science," it was a clear call for a widely interdisciplinary approach to the study of society, guided by "the assumption that all behavior, individual and social, moral and immoral, normal and psychopathic, is generated from the same primary laws."[48] The ground was well prepared for the "behavioral revolution" of the 1950s in which most political scientists rapidly converted to the new "hard science" style.

The use of the term *behavioral* in political science appears to be both an acknowledgement of the debt to the behaviorist movement in psychology and a way of keeping some distance from it, especially from its more radically mechanistic aspects. Much of what is admitted into the realm of "data" in political science—such material as the results of questionnaires—would not be accepted as such by strict behavior psychologists; yet even this kind of information is, as much as possible, ordered and studied in methods resembling those of the "hard sciences."

We examine in later chapters some of the peculiar kinds of political conservatism which creep into behavioral political science, and tend to contradict the idea that behavioralism is value free and ideologically neutral. We will be prepared to do this as long as we understand that one of the chief convictions of the behavioralists is that it *is* value free and non-ideological, that it is scientific method and nothing more. This belief is itself a kind of conservatism: it limits what can be studied, what is taken to be real. Mannheim writes:

> It is not to be denied that the carrying over of the methods of natural science to the social sciences gradually leads to a situation where one no longer asks what one would like to know and what will be of decisive significance for the next step in social development, but attempts to deal only with those complexes of facts which are measurable according to a certain already existent method. Instead of attempting to discover what is most significant with the highest degree of precision possible under the existing circumstances, one tends to be content to attribute importance to what is measurable merely because it happens to be measurable.[49]

Since this statement comes from an admitted critic of the behavioral approach my point might be better made by an advocate. Thus a guide to methodology in social science research warns the scholar against "choosing topics for social research on which . . . there are no valid data or where the basic underlying researches have not been made," and goes on to say: "International relations, strikes and lockouts, poverty and riches are examples of topics heavily weighted with emotions and should, therefore, be carefully considered both from the standpoint of feasibility of obtaining accurate and reliable facts and methods of approach."[50]

Behavioral scholarship has generated a whole vocabulary of terms—"cosmic," "metaphysical," "philosophical," "normative," "personal," "emotional," "subjective"—for shunting aside the things that do not fit its methodology. The tragedy of this particular chapter in the search for human wisdom is that it has convinced a generation of students and scholars that the things people feel and care about most deeply, the problems that most urgently cry out to be solved, are not the proper subjects of their study.

Notes

[1] J. B. Watson, *Behaviorism*, p. 11. Copyright 1924, 1925, 1930 by W. W. Norton & Company, Inc.; Copyright renewed 1952, 1953, 1958 by John B. Watson.

[2] Lasswell calls Freud "a truly scientific spirit who recorded everything of which the human mind was capable, and looked at it critically in the hope of finding the laws of mental life." *Psychopathology and Politics* (see ch. 2, fn. 36), p. 12.

[3]John B. Watson and William McDougall, *The Battle of Behaviorism* (London: Kegan Paul, Trench, Trubner, 1928), pp. 17–19.

[4]E. L. Thorndike, *Animal Intelligence* (New York: Macmillan, 1911).

[5]I. P. Pavlov, *Conditioned Reflexes* (London: Oxford Universsity Press, 1927).

[6]Watson, *Behaviorism*, p. 303 fn.

[7]B. F. Skinner, *The Behavior of Organisms: An Experimental Analysis* (New York: Appleton-Century-Crofts, 1938), p. 47.

[8]Skinner, "Operant Behavior," in *Operant Behavior: Areas of Research and Application* ed. Werner K. Honig (New York: Appleton-Century-Crofts, 1966), pp. 12–32.

[9]B. F. Skinner, *Walden Two* (New York: Macmillan, 1948), p. 262.

[10]Skinner, *Science and Human Behavior* (New York: Macmillan, 1953), p. 9.

[11]*Ibid.*, p. 322.

[12]*Ibid.*, p. 438.

[13]Skinner, *Beyond Freedom and Dignity* (New York: Alfred A. Knopf, Inc. © 1971), p. 172.

[14]*Ibid.*, p. 164.

[15]George Braziller, Inc.—from *The Broken Image* by Floyd W. Matson; reprinted with the permission of the publisher. Copyright © 1964 by Floyd W. Matson. p. 60.

[16]Karl Mannheim, *Man and Society in an Age of Reconstruction* (New York: Harcourt, Brace Jovanovich, Inc., 1940 and Routledge & Kegan Paul Ltd.) p. 213.

[17]*Ibid.*, p. 214.

[18]*Ibid.*, p. 216.

[19]Talcott Parsons, "Definitions of Health and Illness in the Light of American Values and Social Structure," in *Patients, Physicians and Illness* ed. E. Gartley Jaco (Glencoe, Ill.: Free Press, 1963), p. 176.

[20]Richard Sennett, review of *Beyond Freedom and Dignity*, *New York Times Book Review*, 24 Oct 1971, © 1971 by the New York Times Company. Reprinted by permission. p. 1.

[21]*Behaviorism*, p. 297.

[22]Donald M. Baer, "Let's Take Another Look at Punishment," Excerpted from *Psychology Today* Magazine, October 1971. Copyright © Communications/Research/Machines, Inc.

[23]H. J. Eysenck and S. Rachman, *The Causes and Cures of Neurosis* (San Diego: Robert R. Knapp, 1965), p. 3.

[24]*Ibid.*, p. 10.

[25]V. Meyer and Edward W. Chesser, *Behavior Therapy in Clinical Psychiatry* (Middlesex, England: Penguin Books, © 1970), p. 95.

[26]Eysenck and Rachman, *Causes and Cures*, p. 163.

[27]K. Freund, "Some Problems in the Treatment of Homosexuality," in *Behavior Therapy and the Neuroses* ed. H. J. Eysenck (New York: Pergamon Press, 1960), p. 317.

[28]Leonard Kassner, "Assessment of Token Economy Programmes in Psychiatric Hospitals," in *The Role of Learning in Psychotherapy* ed. Ruth Porter (London: 1968), p. 156.

[29]*Ibid.*, p. 157.

[30]*Ibid.*, p. 160.

[31]*Ibid.*, p. 168.

[32]*Ibid.*, p. 169.

[33]*Ibid.*, p. 164.

[34]Thomas Szasz, *Law, Liberty and Psychiatry* (New York: Macmillan, 1963), p. 39.

[35]Ronald Leifer, *In the Name of Mental Health: The Social Functions of Psychiatry* (New York: Science House, 1969), p. 227.

[36]"Another Look at Punishment," p. 32. Italics added.

[37]Meyer and Chesser, *Behavior Therapy*, p. 227. Italics added.

[38]Jessica Mitford, "Kind and Usual Punishment in California," *Atlantic Monthly*, March 1971, p. 47.

[39]H. J. Eysenck, *Crime and Personality* (Boston: Houghton Mifflin, 1964).

[40]Bernard Crick, *American Science of Politics* (Berkeley: University of California Press, 1959), p. v. Originally published by the University of California Press; reprinted by permission of The Regents of the University of California.

[41]Arthur F. Bentley, *The Process of Government: A Study of Social Pressures* (1908), (Evanston,

Ill.: Principia Press, 1935.) A similar argument was being advanced in England, however; see Graham Wallas, *Human Nature in Politics* (1908), (London: A. Constable and Co., Ltd., 1916).

[42]Bentley, *Process of Government*, p. 202.

[43]*Ibid.*, p. 200.

[44]Bentley, *Inquiry into Inquiries: Essays in Social Theory* (Boston: Beacon Press, 1954), p. 32.

[45]Edwin Boring, *A History of Experimental Psychology* (New York: Appleton-Century-Crofts, 1950), p. 645.

[46]Matson, *Broken Image* , p. 83.

[47]*Ibid.*, p. 62.

[48]Clark L. Hull, *Principles of Behavior: An Introduction to Behavior Theory* (New York: Appleton-Century-Crofts, 1943), p. v.

[49]Mannheim, *Ideology and Utopia* (New York: Harcourt, Brace Jovanovich, Inc. 1949 and Routledge & Kegan Paul Ltd.), p. 46.

IV. Self-Actualization and The Social Order

Every age but ours has had its model, its ideal. All these have been given us by our culture; the saint, the hero, the gentleman, the knight, the mystic. About all we have left is the well-adjusted man without problems, a very pale and doubtful substitute. Perhaps we shall soon be able to use as our guide and model the fully growing and self-fulfilling human being, the one in whom all his potentialities are coming to full development, the one whose inner nature expresses itself freely, rather than being warped, suppressed, or denied.

—Abraham H. Maslow[1]

Let us now begin to look at humanistic psychology. Renaissance humanism presented an enthusiastic vision of the possibilities of life, which the people of the times expressed in their art, in their literature, and in their free-wheeling and less-than-scrupulous dealings with one another. Human lives were sometimes treated as works of art, but the art of living never became a science of living, a systematic investigation of the possibilities of human existence. When it did tend toward the systematic, as in Machiavelli's careful search for the basic principles of power, it was so suffused with the rampant opportunism and individualism of the times that it could only produce a set of guidelines for the manipulation of other people. Contemporary humanistic psychologists, working with the advantage of another five centuries of history, are trying again to create an art and science of human existence.

Any science is in part shaped by what its researchers choose to study, by the things that, deliberately or not, they select to be in their line of vision. Abraham Maslow believed that psychologists had allowed themselves to become so preoccupied with mental illness that they had neglected almost entirely to form a meaningful concept of real health, of a fully functioning human being. "It becomes more and more clear," Maslow wrote, "that the study of crippled, stunted, immature, and unhealthy specimens can yield only a cripple psychology and a cripple philosophy."[2]

Maslow—who started out as a behaviorist and became, by the time of his death in 1970, the leading exponent of humanistic psychology—devoted most of the later years of his life to the development of a theory of human health, and to research with healthy (self-actualizing) people. Maslow and his coworkers chose a group of self-actualizing persons to study. They used a rather complex selection process which involved both positive criteria (evidence of use of abilities, gratification of basic

37

emotional needs, sense of self-esteem) and negative criteria (absence of neurosis, psychosis, psychosomatic illness).

Self-actualization, Maslow confessed, was a rather difficult syndrome to describe at the early stages. In general terms, it meant:

> . . . the full use and exploitation of talents, capacities, potentialities, etc. Such people seem to be fulfilling themselves and to be doing the best that they are capable of doing, reminding us of Neitzsche's exhortation, "Become what thou art." They are people who have developed or are developing to the full stature of which they are capable. . . . These potentialities may be either idosyncratic or species-wide. . . . [3]

Although the subjects showed a wide range of personality characteristics, certain patterns did begin to emerge from the research. Maslow found that his subjects had many characteristics in common; among them:

Efficient perception of reality.

Acceptance of self, of others and of nature.

Spontaneity.

Problem-centering (rather than ego-centering).

Detachment and desire for privacy.

Autonomy and resistance to enculturation.

Continued freshness of appreciation, and richness of emotional reactions.

Frequency of peak or mystical experiences.

Identification with the human species *(Gemeinschaftsgefühl)*.

Deep interpersonal relations.

Democratic character structure.

Greatly increased creativeness.

Certain changes in the value system. [4]

Maslow eventually became convinced that the study of self-actualizing people was producing not only a better conceptualization of mental health, but a whole new psychology, a radically different vision of humanity. He posited the following as some of its basic assertions:

1. We have, each of us, an essential biologically based inner nature, which is to some degree "natural," intrinsic, given, and, in a certain limited sense, unchangeable, or, at least, unchanging.
2. Each person's inner nature is in part unique to himself and in part species-wide.
3. It is possible to study this inner nature scientifically and to discover what it is like (not *invent—discover*).
4. This inner nature, as much as we know of it so far, seems not to be intrinsically evil, but rather either neutral or positively "good."

What we call evil behavior appears most often to be a secondary reaction to frustration of this intrinsic nature.

5. Since this inner nature is good or neutral rather than bad, it is best to bring it out and to encourage it rather than to suppress it. If it is permitted to guide our life, we grow healthy, fruitful, and happy.

6. If this essential core of the person is denied or suppressed, he gets sick sometimes in obvious ways, sometimes in subtle ways, sometimes immediately, sometimes later.

7. This inner nature is not strong and overpowering and unmistakable like the instincts of animals. It is weak and delicate and subtle and easily overcome by habit, cultural pressure, and wrong attitudes toward it.

8. Even though weak, it rarely disappears in the normal person— perhaps not even in the sick person. Even though denied, it persists underground forever pressing for actualization.

9. Somehow, these conclusions must all be articulated with the necessity of discipline, deprivation, frustration, pain, and tragedy. To the extent that these experiences reveal and foster and fulfill our inner nature, to that extent they are desirable experiences.[5]

Obviously, if Maslow's idea of humanity has any psychological validity at all, then it must have sociological and political validity as well. Some application of his psychology to other fields was fairly explicit in Maslow's work. Consider, for example, his statement about the "resistance to enculturation" of the self-actualizing person:

Such a person, by virtue of what he has become, assumes a new relation to his society and, indeed, to society in general. He not only transcends himself in various ways; he also transcends his culture. He resists enculturation. He becomes more detached from his culture and from his society. He becomes a little more a member of his species and a little less a member of his local group. My feeling is that most sociologists and anthropologists will take this hard.[6]

He might have added political scientists to the list of people who would take it hard. The idea that healthy human growth tends toward de-enculturation adds a new dimension to some of the basic concepts of political philosophy, such as obligation and authority. It also opens up new areas for empirical research: behavioral political scientists have done a good deal of research on socialization—how the social order gets built into the individual—but have made no comparable investigation of any process of de-socialization. But Maslow clearly means that the "transcendence of culture" is a kind of desocialization: self-actualizing people simply outgrow much of what they have been taught about society and their relation to it.

Maslow did not find that his self-actualizing subjects were authority rebels or even particularly unconventional in their daily behavior, yet they were quite capable of rebellion or unconventionality:

The expressed inner attitude is usually that it is ordinarily of no great consequence which folkways are used, that one set of traffic rules is as good as any other set, that while they make life smoother they do not really matter enough to make a fuss about. . . .

But since this tolerant acceptance is not warm approval with identification, their yielding to convention is apt to be rather casual and perfunctory. . . . In the pinches, when yielding to conventions is too annoying or too expensive, the apparent conventionality reveals itself for the superficial thing that it is, and is tossed off as easily as a cloak.[7]

It is interesting to me that Maslow did not consider this particular facet of the character structure of self-actualizing people to be of outstanding importance; he merely mentioned it as one of several points to be considered. Personally I find it a revolutionary idea. It says that there exist within our society a significant number of people—some of our wisest and strongest, in fact—who are "in" the society in a fundamentally different way from the rest of us. The attitude of these people toward some of the things that civilizations traditionally rest upon— cultural norms, laws, etc.—seems to be that they are all right if you keep them in their place.

This amounts to a roughly stated hypothesis about the relationship between the type of consciousness which has been reached by an individual and the way in which that individual perceives the social order and operates within it. This idea has been taken up by others, and we will deal with a fairly sophisticated elaboration of it—a theory of psychosocial development—in chapter 9. At this point I would like to mention one important thing about Maslow's work. Although he found self-actualizing subjects quite capable of radical social action, such action was not a result of deprivation, commonly assumed to be the main source of revolutionary social change, nor was it the acting out of personal pathology according to the Freudian model.

Because this finding is so different from our conventional ideas about motivation, Maslow in several of his later works found it necessary to differentiate between two kinds of motivation: one is *deficiency-motivation*, the drive of the organism to acquire whatever it lacks for survival (food, safety, etc.); the other is *being-motivation* or "metamotivation," the drive of those individuals who have taken care of the basic deficiency needs. The latter form of behavior, of course, is that of healthy or self-actualizing people. "The most highly developed persons we know are metamotivated to a much higher degree, and are basic-need motivated to a lesser degree, than average or diminished people are."[8]

The idea of a hierarchy of needs was one of Maslow's basic contributions to psychological theory, and it clarifies what he means by metamotivation. This system recognizes five main categories:

1. Physiological needs—food, water, shelter, sex, sleep, etc.
2. Safety needs—order, stability.
3. Belongingness and love needs.
4. Esteem needs—self-respect, and respect from others.
5. Self-actualization needs.[9]

The system is hierarchical; its thesis is that higher needs will tend to emerge and demand the attention of the organism as the more basic needs are satisfied. When physiological needs are taken care of, the individual will proceed to the satisfaction of safety needs—from there to love and affection needs, and so forth. Conversely, the more the basic needs remain unfulfilled, the less likely will the individual be to direct his or her attention and energies to the satisfaction of higher needs. But, and this is one of Maslow's central ideas, the so-called higher needs are still biologically inherent in the human being, different only in order of precedence from those drives usually designated as instincts. The altruistic, creative behavior of self-actualizing men and women is, in Maslow's view, the natural satisfaction of complex biological needs.

The image of the self-actualizing person which emerges from Maslow's research is quite different from the traditional idea of the self-denying idealist; Maslow's subjects tended to be both altruistic and hedonistic. They were hearty enjoyers of food, sex, etc., and at the same time genuinely and effectively committed to goals of total human progress, operating out of a highly developed sense of membership in the species. They did not act in denial of their own needs, but in fulfillment of them.

We should note here the difference between Maslow and behaviorist theory. The behaviorists recognize a variety of needs, some capable of taking precedence over others, but not a hierarchy; there is no concept of more complex needs arising within the organism as basic needs are satisfied. Behaviorists stress the techniques of controlling organisms by manipulating the environment (selective satisfaction or frustration of needs) but do not recognize the possibility that the growing organism might assume a different kind of relationship to its environment. The idea of self-actualization is characteristically humanistic because it describes possibilities of growth which are characteristically human, which one would not be likely to discover in the study of rats and pigeons.

Although Maslow saw the higher needs as emerging naturally out of the same biological source as the lower ones, he did not see them as simply lower needs in disguise. Thus he insisted that love had to be recognized as a human need in its own right. Love, for the Freudians, is derived from sex. "The most widely accepted of the various theories put forth by Freud," Maslow noted, "is that tenderness is aim-inhibited sexuality."[10] And love, he added, is more or less boycotted by scientific psychologists:

One might reasonably expect that the writers of serious treatises on the family, on marriage, and on sex should consider the subject of love to be a proper, even basic, part of their self-imposed task. But I must report that no single one of the volumes on these subjects available in the library where I work has any serious mention of the subject. More often, the word love is not even indexed.[11]

Maslow's point of view, which in this respect is fairly representative of humanistic psychology in general, holds love to be a natural human drive (which may or may not be related to sex) requiring satisfaction in order for the individual to proceed toward realization of his or her potential. Conversely, the failure to satisfy love and belongingness needs contributes to mental illness: "In our society the thwarting of these needs is the most commonly found core in cases of maladjustment and more severe psychopathology."[12]

Although Maslow's thinking carried him a long way from his behaviorist beginnings, his work lends itself fairly well to empirical research. Several attempts have been made to test it out and to relate it to other social science research. One early effort in this direction was made by James C. Davies.[13]

Davies correlated Maslow's system with existing research to show how political behavior may be affected by the level of basic need satisfaction. For example, researchers at the University of Minnesota placed a group of subjects on a semistarvation diet for a period of twenty-four weeks, and found increasing apathy, a lessening ability to concentrate on anything except the dominant need for food, and a loss of self-confidence as expressed by one subject who wished that the people controlling the experiment would "put strong checks on us."[14]

This laboratory research corroborated various reports of what happens to individuals during famines or in concentration camps: "Extreme hunger, as starvation approaches, produces apathy and manipulability. People become too weak and too busy staying alive to take either strong or concerted action against government."[15] And it has been found that other kinds of basic physiological deprivation—such as lack of sleep—contribute to the manipulability of people, permit them to be deliberately brainwashed by authorities into acceptance of new political ideologies.[16]

Thus for people whose most basic physiological needs have not been met, political action—even an organized and sustained drive to obtain food—is not possible. At a higher level on the need hierarchy, Davies saw political action as both demanding and providing some fulfillment of *social* needs:

Satisfaction of the physical needs is a condition precedent for politics; existence of the social needs is both a condition precedent and a condition concurrent. People become involved in public affairs both because some of their social needs have been otherwise met and because they find *some* inherent social satisfaction in political involvement.

Some satisfaction of the social needs in other than political ways is thus probably necessary to make it possible for people to take part in the process of deciding what are the common goals of their society and how best to achieve them.[17]

However, this work is still only a very partial exploration of the political meaning of the need-hierarchy theory. It brings in research findings which tend to substantiate the hypothesis that deprivation of needs at one level interferes with the emergence of drives at the higher levels. But there are only scattered indications that if the basic needs are met the progress to higher needs, the growth, will in fact take place. A humanistic political science must pay attention to the presence of growth as well as to its absence. Also, the research findings and the theoretical interpretation are most clear and meaningful at the lower levels of the need hierarchy, especially at the lowest. At the higher levels research becomes scantier, and terminology becomes less clear; love and belongingness are absorbed into a general category of "social needs," and self-actualization becomes only a higher kind of consumerism:

> There is one sense in which perhaps the large majority of people do relate their political participation to self-actualization. On any comparative basis it is clear that the standard of living in the industrialized Western world is high and that people, by and large, are relatively secure in what they have. Yet they want more and sometimes seek more through their government. The relatively poor Frenchman who seeks a higher housing subsidy, the similar American who votes for the candidate who advocates a higher minimum wage or shorter hours, and any citizen who votes for a candidate who promises a reduction in personal income taxes are all well-off when compared with the unindustrialized, poor, and politically inactive Persian or Arab.
>
> In these situations, the motivation appears to be related indirectly to the need for self-actualization, in the sense that they want a better living standard and more security generally. . . . [18]

This description does not show what Maslow meant by self-actualization. But the weakness is more a characteristic of political science generally than of Davies' specific attempt to apply a humanistic psychologist's system to politics. Political scientists as a whole are considerably more at ease when explaining political behavior in terms of the more primitive human drives. The complex human motivations of which Maslow speaks do not lend themselves easily to the popular techniques of quantification—and I do not think their absence from political science can be explained merely in terms of methodology. It seems to me, rather, that there is a kind of invisible taboo in the social sciences against undue attention to anything which might smack of impracticality or idealism; the social scientist wants desperately to be a practical, realistic person and to be respected in the world of practical and realistic people.

It is interesting to note that Davies' book, which was published in 1963, contains in its list of sources only two articles by Maslow, both published in the early forties.[19] Although there is discussion of self-actualization as a higher need, there is no discussion whatever of the self-actualization syndrome or of the attempt to work toward a psychology of health—which were amply explained by Maslow in his own book, *Motivation and Personality*, published in 1954. It is even more interesting to note that the chapter in *Motivation and Personality* which puts forth the self-actualization theory was based on an earlier paper. In the preface to the book Maslow said, "This paper was written about 1943 but it was seven years before I summoned up enough courage to print it."[20]

Maslow, at any rate, did eventually sum up the courage to publish his ideas about self-actualization and the hierarchy of needs. Much of his lifework, in fact, amounts to a virtual crusade to turn the attention of the American scientific and academic establishment toward the systematic study of the possibilities of growth, to convince them that the higher needs—metaneeds—are a true and accessible part of human reality:

These metaneeds, though having certain special characteristics which differentiate them from basic needs, are yet in the same realm of discourse and of research as, for instance, the need for vitamin C or for calcium. They are certainly *not* the exclusive property of theologians, philosphers, or artists. The spiritual or value-life then falls well *within* the realm of nature, rather than being a different and opposed realm. It is susceptible to investigation at once by psychologists and social scientists, and in theory will eventually become also a problem for neurology, endocrinology, genetics, and biochemistry as these sciences develop suitable methods.[21]

Maslow was convinced that the failure to recognize such needs and possibilities contributed to the "frustrated idealism" experienced by many young people, particularly students:

This frustrated idealism and occasional hopelessness is partially due to the influence and ubiquity of stupidly limited theories of motivation all over the world. Leaving aside behavioristic and positivistic theories—or rather, non-theories—as simple refusals even to see the problem, i.e., a kind of psychoanalytic denial, then what is available to the idealistic young man and woman?

Not only does the whole of official nineteenth-century science and orthodox academic psychology offer him nothing, but also the major motivation theories by which most men live can lead him only to depression or cynicism. The Freudians, at least in their official writings (though not in good therapeutic practice), are still reductionistic about all higher human values. The deepest and most real motivations are seen to be dangerous and nasty, while the highest human values are essentially fake, being not what they seem to be, but camouflaged versions of the "deep, dark, and dirty." Our social scientists are just as disappointing in the main. A total cultural determinism is still the official, orthodox doctrine of many or most of the sociologists and anthropologists. This doctrine not only denies intrinsic higher motivations, but comes perilously close sometimes to denying "human nature" itself. The economists, not only in the West but also in the East, are essentially materialistic. We must say harshly of the "science" of economics that it is generally the skilled, exact, technological application of a totally false theory of human needs and values, a theory which recognizes only the existence of lower needs or material needs.[22]

Maslow did not go far in the direction of stating the social or political theories which might be derived from his work—that job still remains to be done—but he did outline some ideas about his conceptualization of a healthy (he called it synergic or Eupsychian) society. This outline was in part a logical extrapolation of his interest in full health and development in the individual, and in part an elaboration on some of the later anthropological work of Ruth Benedict. Benedict had distinguished between "low synergy" societies and "high synergy" societies, the latter being those which "have social orders in which the individual, by the same act and at the same time, serves his own advantage and that of the group."[23] Maslow, applying her criteria to American society, found it to be of mixed synergy; capable in some areas of fulfilling needs and facilitating personal growth; in other areas tending to frustrate needs and stunt development, to pit people unnecessarily against each other or against society itself.

Although Maslow's political theory is not highly developed, its two main propositions come through clearly. These are (1) that, contrary to Freudian theory, the needs of people and the needs of civilization are not *necessarily* antagonistic and (2) that the possibilities of a society's development are contingent upon the ability of its structures and its members to recognize and encourage higher human needs and the potential for self-actualization. Therefore, social science, political dialogue, and public policy must recognize and deal with needs other than the more basic material ones.

These two propostions are workable guidelines, I believe, toward the development of humanistic politics and a humanistic political science.

Notes

[1] *Toward a Psychology of Being* (see ch. 1, fn. 14), p. 4.
[2] A. H. Maslow, *Motivation and Personality* (New York: Harper and Row, 1954), p. 180.
[3] *Ibid.*, pp. 200–201.
[4] *Ibid.*, p. 203 ff.
[5] *Toward a Psychology of Being*, pp. 3–4.
[6] *Ibid.*, p. 11.
[7] *Motivation and Personality*, p. 225.
[8] Maslow, "A Theory of Metamotivation: The Biological Rooting of the Value-Life," *Journal of Humanistic Psychology*, Fall 1967, p. 105.
[9] *Motivation and Personality*. p. 80 ff.
[10] *Ibid.*, p. 247. Maslow cited Freud, *Civilization and Its Discontents*, p. 22; M. Balint, "On Genital Love," *Intern. J. Psychoanalysis* (1948) 29: 34–40; and Edward Hitchmann, "Freud's Conception of Love," *Intern. J. Psychoanalysis* (1952), 33: 1–8.
[11] *Ibid.*, p. 235.
[12] *Ibid.*, p. 89.
[13] James C. Davies, *Human Nature in Politics* (New York: Wiley, 1963).
[14] Reports of the research are in Ancel Keys et al., *The Biology of Human Starvation* (Minneapolis: U. of Minnesota Press, 1950) and in J. Brozek, "Semi-Starvation and Nutritional Rehabilitation," *Journal of Clinical Nutrition* (1953), 1: 107–108.
[15] Davies, *Human Nature*, p. 15.
[16] See, for example, Robert Jay Lifton, *Thought Reform and the Psychology of Totalism* (New York: W. W. Norton, 1961).
[17] Davies, *Human Nature*, p. 34.
[18] *Ibid.*, pp. 55–56.
[19] "The Dynamics of Psychological Security-Insecurity," *Character and Personality* (1942), 10: 331–344; "A Theory of Human Motivation," *Psychological Review* (1943), 50: 370–396.
[20] *Motivation and Personality*, p. xiii.
[21] Maslow, "A Theory of Metamotivation: The Biological Rooting of the Value-Life," *Journal of Humanistic Psychology* (1967), 2: 109–110.
[22] *Ibid.*, p. 110.
[23] Maslow, "Synergy in the Society and in the Individual," *Journal of Individual Psychology* (1964), 20. See also Frank Goble, *Third Force*.

V. Gestalt: Futureshock Therapy

The previously robotized corpses begin to return to life, gaining substance and beginning the dance of abandonment and self-fulfillment; the paper people are turning into real people.

—Frederick Perls[1]

As we proceed to gestalt therapy we are moving into a system that places great value upon the subjective, experiential aspects of learning. For the first time in this book we will encounter the idea—which runs through much of humanistic psychology—that a firm grasp of the theory and relevant data about some experience is not necessarily knowledge of the experience itself, and may in fact be a form of ignorance. This idea often gets humanistic psychologists accused of being anti-intellectual. The accusation is, in my opinion, true but only partly true: humanistic psychologists are for the most part card-carrying intellectuals themselves, and their position seems to be that intellectual comprehension is one way toward achieving understanding, but is not understanding in itself. Real human growth cannot be taught or learned; it can only be done, and perhaps, with luck, one can be helped to find things out for oneself. Data and wisdom are not synonymous.

So keep in mind that gestalt therapy is primarily a lot of experiences, things that at this moment are happening between people and within people. Around those experiences has grown up a body of theory and literature, some of which is excellent and some of which is not so good. (A collaborator of the late Fritz Perls, the founder of gestalt therapy, recently said that he was a great guy but not much of one to write a book.[2]) The main existing works on gestalt therapy are cited in this chapter, but I strongly recommend that, if you find gestalt interesting, you obtain some personal experience or instruction in it before going too far into the literature. Otherwise you run the risk of becoming an expert, and most gestaltists believe that there is nobody more out of it than an expert.

Although gestalt is a uniquely contemporary and American form of psychotherapy, it is also a blend of many influences: Freud, the neo-Freudians, Reich, Moreno, gestalt psychology, existentialism, holism, Zen Buddhism. Frederick, or Fritz, Perls was first a Freudian, but he was also exposed to research in gestalt psychology during a period of work with Kurt Goldstein in the 1920s. His analyst at the time he left Germany in 1933 was Wilhelm Reich, who was then developing his own theory of "character armor." He met Jan Christian Smuts in Frankfurt and was impressed by Smuts' book, *Holism and Evolution*. Perls lived and worked in South Africa for many years, and came to the United States in

1946; his own form of therapy developed through the forties, fifties, and sixties. In 1964 he began a period of residence at the Esalen Institute at Big Sur—and gestalt began to grow rapidly; it is now listed as the sixth most common affiliation among American psychotherapists, exceeding such older or more-published schools as the Jungian and the rational-emotive.[3]

Gestalt *psychology* was not a therapeutic system but rather an experimental-theoretical orientation concerned mainly with sense perceptions (especially visual) and the ways the human brain organizes sensory data into perceptual units (gestalten). The idea that the whole of something is greater than the sum of its parts is a fairly accurate statement of the main theme of gestalt psychology; Max Wertheimer's formulation was: "There are wholes, the behavior of which is not determined by that of their individual elements, but where the part-processes are themselves determined by the intrinsic nature of the whole."[4]

At the Institute for Brain-Damaged Soldiers in Frankfurt, where Perls was briefly employed, Kurt Goldstein was carrying gestalt psychology into new realms; he was studying the ways in which seriously maimed human beings could learn to reorganize themselves to function again. It was during this period, Perls has said, that he first began to think of the human organism as a whole, as something more than an agglomeration of characteristics.[5]

The therapeutic system which Perls eventually developed looks at every human being as a totality: emotions, thoughts, sense perceptions, physical actions are intricately interrelated factors. Further, it looks at the organism as a figure against the ground of a larger whole; the patient is always dealt with in his or her actual, present, here-and-now environment.

The healthy organism, to the gestalt way of thinking, lives in a flowing, ever-changing balance with its environment; it is aware of what goes on around it and sensitive to its own needs; it takes in what it requires and rejects what it cannot use; when a need emerges the organism moves to satisfy it; when the need is satisfied, the need recedes from consciousness and the organism is open to whatever comes next. The organism is an integrated, harmonious whole. Its parts are not at war with one another.

Less healthy human organisms—psychotic, neurotic, or simply less than fully functioning individuals—are likely to be fragmented, seriously out of touch with their own senses of sight and touch and taste and smell, only vaguely aware of their own bodies and what they are doing, similarly unaware of many of their own needs—which are, if recognized at all, felt to be shameful or somehow inappropriate. Such individuals seldom exist fully "in the now," but are continually fighting rearguard actions with the unfinished business of the past or dealing in fantasy with the threats and promises of the future. One of the most common routes of escape from reality is into the never-never-land of words; life can be fluently talked *about*, but rarely experienced.

The most important concepts in gestalt are awareness and integration. The following passage, which appears early in the basic text on gestalt therapy, indicates how these two tie together:

Awareness is characterized by *contact*, by *sensing*, by *excitement* and by Gestalt formation. Its adequate functioning is the real of normal psychology; any disturbance comes under the heading of psychopathology.

Contact as such is possible without awareness, but for awareness contact is indispensable. The crucial question is: with what is one in contact? The spectator of a modern painting may believe that he is in contact with the picture while he is actually in contact with the art critic of his favorite journal.

Sensing determines the nature of awareness, whether distant (e.g., acoustic), close (e.g., tactile) or within the skin (proprioceptive). In the last term is included the sensing of one's own dreams and thoughts.   *Excitement* covers the physiological excitation as well as the undifferentiated emotions.

Gestalt formation always accompanies awareness. We do not see three isolated points, we make a triangle out of them. The formation of complete and comprehensive Gestalten is the condition of mental health and growth. Only the completed Gestalt can be organized as an automatically functioning unit in the total organism. Any incomplete Gestalt represents an "unfinished situation" that clamors for attention and interferes with the formation of any novel, vital Gestalt. Instead of growth and development we then find stagnation and repression.[6]

The aim of gestalt therapy is not so much a cure of sickness, in the medical sense, as an awakening; the successful product of gestalt work literally sees the world more clearly and feels his or her own mind, body, and emotions operating as an integrated whole.

Gestalt therapy differs from Freudian analysis in that no attempt is made to delve into the past for clues to the origins of problems. Rather, it stresses the fact that the difficulties, whatever they are, exist in the here and now. The effort is to help patients get in touch with *what* they do and *how* they do it. Searching for answers to the *why* questions, the gestaltist believes, lures both patient and therapist down a long—and costly—byway from which they may never return to any true confrontation with what is going on in the present.

Gestalt differs from behavior therapy in that—although change is expected to come about—there is no direct effort to alter behavior. The emphasis is not on what patients should do, but on what they do—what strategies they employ for manipulating people, what bodily feelings they experience at certain times, what situations they seek out and what situations they avoid. This emphasis has been called "the paradoxical theory of change":

Change occurs when one becomes what he is, not when he tries to become what he is not. Change does not take place through a coercive attempt by the individual or by another person to change him, but it does take place if one takes the time and effort to be what he is—to be fully invested in his current positions. By rejecting the role of change agent, we make meaningful and orderly change possible.[7]

This process of going deeply into the actual present situation may involve a good deal of work and a variety of therapeutic techniques. The following list of the gestalt "injunctions" gives the basic guidelines, equally applicable to the therapy session or to the patient's ongoing life style:

1. Live now. Be concerned with the present rather than with past or future.
2. Live here. Deal with what is present rather than with what is absent.
3. Stop imagining. Experience the real.
4. Stop unnecessary thinking. Rather, taste and see.
5. Express rather than manipulate, explain, justify or judge.
6. Give in to unpleasantness and pain just as to pleasure. Do not restrict your awareness.
7. Accept no *should* or *ought* other than your own. Adore no graven image.
8. Take full responsibility for your actions, feelings, and thoughts.
9. Surrender to being as you are.[8]

These instructions sound easy enough, but the actual practice of gestalt work reveals that everyone has an enormous hidden arsenal of defenses against experiencing reality—and the most formidable of these is the ability to conceal from oneself the very fact that such defenses exist. Patients in gestalt may well get into touch with a rich world of sensual and physical sensation, but first they will have to recognize and experience their own defenses against awareness. They will, in many ways, come face to face with themselves, and will confront their ways of escaping from the uncertain, threatening world of the here and now. If the therapy is to be successful, they will have to "own" their projective and avoidance techniques, come to think of themselves less as victims, and take responsibility for what goes on in their lives. Gestalt therapy talks a great deal about responsibility, but it has a meaning rather different from the traditional moral exhortation to take responsibility for oneself. The gestaltist is convinced that all people already are responsible for most of what is happening to them, but simply unaware of how they manipulate the environment and simultaneously block their own awareness of what they are doing. The following passage gives some sense of this, and also brings us toward the political meaning of gestalt:

The attitude of the passive-suffering projector . . . we believe is typical of modern dissociated man. It is imbedded in our language, our world-attitude, our institutions. The prevention of outgoing motion and initiative, the social derogation of aggressive drives, and the epidemic disease of self-control and self-conquest have led to a language in which the self seldom does or expresses anything; instead, "it" happens. These restrictive measures have also led to a view of the world as completely neutral and "objective" and unrelated to our concerns; and to institutions that take over our functions, that are to "blame" because they "control" us, and that wreak on us the hostility which we so carefully refrain from wielding ourselves—as if men did not themselves lend to institutions whatever force they have![9]

The gestalt view of internalized social norms is quite similar to Freud's theory of the introjected superego, which guards over the psyche "like a garrison in a conquered city." This internalization creates within people a resistance to taking conscious responsibility for their own actions and emotions. Their stronger drives, sexual and aggressive, become alien to them and are experienced as projections—instead of owning their anger and violence, they believe the world around them to be angry and violent. The gestalt picture of people embattled against the phantoms that represent their own inner drives can easily be enlarged to a view of the world divided into paranoid nations proclaiming peace while arming endlessly against the aggressiveness of the others.

This idea of a close relationship between authority and awareness is one of the major contributions of gestalt. It gives us a clinical perspective on a psychological principle that seems to be understood by a growing number of political activists. The principle can be stated this way: *individuals under the control of an authority not only surrender their own power to that authority but to some extent surrender also their awareness of being controlled.* This principle adds an important, somewhat Kafkaesque twist to the Freudian picture of the superego as a garrison in a conquered city: in the gestalt version, the garrison is becoming invisible; the city thinks it is free.

The political version of the gestalt "paradoxical theory of change" could be stated this way: *to become fully aware of being dominated is itself a step toward ending domination.* This principle, which requires some idea of an internalized component of the authority, appears to be influencing a good deal of contemporary radical action. Women's liberation forces especially are aware of the tremendous potential of "consciousness raising"—bringing the power relationship out into the open—as a technique for social change. I suspect that we will see a good deal more of such action if and when the gestalt theory of change, and its social implications, becomes more widely understood.

Gestalt—for all the scantiness of its theoretical writings and especially of its political content—already appears to be having a significant influence in American life. Theodore Roszak cites gestalt, by way of Paul Goodman (a coauthor of *Gestalt Psychotherapy*), as one of the main ideological resources of the youthful counterculture. "Gestalt," Roszak observes, "is one of the few schools of psychiatry that has been prepared to set society at large into the therapeutic scales and to find the way of the world wanting, a mad attack upon human potentialities. Gestalt holds out for the inherent sociability of the whole human being, including his sexual and even his aggressive needs."[10]

There is a strong case for anarchy in gestalt. It rests on the belief that the creators and enforcers of official rules of behavior—law and order—are operating in total ignorance of real and natural regulatory forces which already exist among people. Perls said:

The anarchy which is usually feared by the controllers is not an anarchy which is without meaning. On the contrary, it means the organism is left alone to take care of itself, without being meddled with from outside. And I believe that this is the great thing to understand: *that awareness per se—by and of itself—can be curative.* Because with full awareness you become aware of this organismic self-regulation, you can let the organism take over without interfering, without interrupting; we can rely on the wisdom of the organism. And the contrast to this is the whole pathology of self-manipulation, environmental control, and so on, that interferes with this subtle organismic self-control.[11]

It is important to understand that when Perls spoke of self-control he was not talking about control of the self by the internalized social rules but rather by deeper, biologically rooted drives that naturally operate to keep the organism functioning in its environment as a balanced system. "Every external control, even *internalized* external control . . . interferes with the healthy working of the organism."[12] Thus in therapy a behavioral pattern is not approached in terms of cultural norms. Adjustment is not the goal:

That our life is not consistent with the demands of society is not because nature is at fault or we are at fault, but because society and the needs of nature do not fit together any more. Again and again we come into such conflict until it becomes doubtful whether a healthy and fully sane and honest person can exist in our insane society.[13]

Here is the point at which therapy appears to fall into step with revolution. In the tension between the needs of individuals and the demands of society, political conservatism in all its forms—law enforcement, traditional morality, and most kinds of psychotherapy—asks people to recognize the unsocial character of their needs, to practice self-control or submit to society's power to control them. Now gestalt says that it is society that is pathological and that must give way so humanity can grow.

Yet I do not know of a single gestalt therapist who is also a political revolutionary, and I do not think this fact can be explained away simply by saying that they are all comfortable professionals and reluctant to expose themselves to the risks of radical activism. Rather, I think they regard their therapy as in itself a revolution, likely to be more meaningful and lasting than the transformation of institutional structures.

Nothing in the theory of internalized controls claims that simply removing the external institutional support of these controls would turn all people into autonomous, responsible, integrated, self-regulating individuals. We can speculate that it might do that for those individuals who were already closer to personal autonomy—or for all people over a period of time—but we can also guess that there would also be outbursts of irrational aggressiveness and surrender to new forms of authority. The internalized controls would soon incarnate themselves again in new externalized controls. In this view political revolution unaccompanied by psychological growth becomes a kind of hacking away at heads of Hydra.

We can find ample historical support for this point of view. Consider the French Revolution which produced, among other things, massive murders, a variety of attempts to enforce morality, several dictatorships, and eventually a hereditary military monarchy. Or the Russian revolution, which abandoned the Marxian ideal of the withering away of the state and settled into dreary bureaucracy, puritanical morality, and international power politics.

Perls, a short time before his death, told gestalt therapists that they had a certain kind of historical mission, which was to make a real revolution possible:

> As you know, there is a rebellion on in the United States. We discover that producing things, and living for things, and the exchange of things, is not the ultimate meaning of life. We discover that the meaning of life is that it is to be lived, and it is not to be traded and conceptualized and squeezed into a pattern of systems. We realize that manipulation and control are not the ultimate joy in life.
>
> But we must also realize that so far we only have a rebellion. We don't have a revolution yet. There is still much of substance missing. . . . I've got plenty of contact with the youngsters of our generation who are in despair. . . . They want to get something out of life. They want to become real and exist. If there is any chance of interrupting the rise and fall of the United States, it's up to our youth and it's up to you in supporting this youth. To be able to do this, there is only one way through: to become real, to learn to take a stand, to develop one's center. . . . [14]

For Perls, then, the work of gestalt was a person-by-person revolution, freeing individuals from their own inner tyranny and fragmentation, paving the way for profound social change. For another gestaltist, Arnold Beisser, the development of personal autonomy is simply a way of dealing with the frightening transience of social systems and values:

> For the first time in the history of mankind, the length of the individual life span is greater than the length of time necessary for major social and cultural change to take place. Moreover, the rapidity with which this change occurs is accelerating. . . . Confronted with a pluralistic, multifaceted, changing system, the individual is left to his own devices to find stability. He must do this through an approach that allows him to move dynamically and flexibly with the times while still maintaining some central gyroscope to guide him. He can no longer do this with ideologies, which become obsolete, but must do it with a change theory, whether explicit or implicit. The goal of therapy becomes not so much to develop a good, fixed character but to be able to move with the times while retaining some individual stability. [15]

There is no point in debating which of these two more accurately represents the political program of gestalt, because gestalt has no political program. Yet I believe that gestalt has important political relevance. It springs out of a profound awareness of the fact that all our social structures exist not simply "out there" in the world of power but also "in here" in the half-hidden politics of the mind. Its assurance that there exists in every person an accessible natural and sane source of self-regulation offers the hope that we can all become, like Maslow's self-actualizing subjects, a little less members of our culture and a little more members of our species.

My own hypothesis about the revolutionary meaning of gestalt is based on my conviction that (1) gestalt therapy is not merely a lonely offshoot in our culture but rather a response to the real and deeply felt needs of many people; and (2) that the gestalt therapists have no monopoly on de-enculturation—that similar kinds of change are being experienced by many people, in and out of therapy. If this hypothesis is true, it means that the psychological foundations of social control are eroding, and that the kind of enforced morality we have always known and accepted in America will no longer be possible. To talk of political revolution as we have known it becomes irrelevant to our times. Nobody will have to overthrow the state; we will simply outgrow our need for many of its functions.

I suspect that the rapid growth of gestalt therapy can be understood by looking at it as a system which has arisen in response to the need of many people to find some way of dealing with the phenomenon of cultural change. Fundamentally there are only two ways of dealing with change. One is to deny it, to surround oneself with familiar things and seek consolation in whatever signs of social stability there are to be found. The other is to take an existential leap into the here and now and face the future as it comes. For decades now existential philosophers have urged us all to take that leap into the precarious reality of the moment, to obey Nietzche's exhortation to "become what thou art," but until quite recently there was no system which claimed to be able to help people develop the kind of inner autonomy which would make such cultural flexibility possible. Gestalt is a technology of existentialism.

Gestalt as Methodology

So far I have been talking mostly in terms of the relevance of gestalt to cultural norms and cultural change. I would like to turn now to the question of how the gestalt perspective can be utilized in political science research.

Gestalt theory, as I have said, is distrustful of abstraction—and that includes its own; training in gestalt therapy is heavily experiential. Therapists are encouraged to see their patients as people and not as the possessors of this or that set of textbook symptoms. Complex psychiatric jargon is rarely heard, and its use is often taken to mean that the therapist is more in touch with the theory than with the patient.

This same value system is transferable to political analysis. Like the art lover who is in contact with a critic and not with the painting, a student of politics may see the legal structures and not the people, the theory but not the fact, the ideology but not the reality. In this respect gestalt has much in common with the pioneers of behavioral research in political science, who believed that the discipline was far too concerned with legalisms and formal structures and philosophical constructs, and virtually blind to the real human behavior that was taking place every day in the world of politics.

But although behavioralism and gestalt spring from a common recognition of a problem, they are diametrically opposed in their ways of looking for the truth. Behavioralists, probably unaware that there was any alternative to be considered, chose the route of dealing with data. To study behavior meant to search for "units" of behavior; researchers were taught to look closely at rigorously fenced-off subjects, to measure, to quantify facts. And, again without any real debate on the matter, certain kinds of behavior were taken to be significant and worthy of research; others were dismissed as irrelevant or simply unmeasurable.

Gestalt, on the other hand, is a *holistic approach*, and this term has a very special meaning in reference to research. Holistic research is not the same thing as "macro" political research; it does not simply mean that one looks at the "big picture." Rather it means that one develops awareness so as to take in as much as possible of what is happening in whatever is being observed; this awareness includes emotions and their physical expression.

In gestalt therapy a great deal of attention is paid to the subtle physical indicators of emotional states: the rigid neck, the clenched fist, the facial expression, the grasping hand, the kicking foot. The therapist directs attention to these, encourages patients to experience the actions as things *they are doing* which express something of what they feel at the moment, what they are trying to say. When the technique is successful the patient becomes aware of the blocked action—often with a rush of feeling—and then is able to move through the impasse and say what he or she means.

The gestalt therapist develops—must develop—a heightened awareness of the ever-chainging flow of emotion, of how it is expressed and how it is blocked. This kind of awareness includes a keen observation of behavior, but it is different from the disciplined objectivity of the behavioral researcher; it is a subjective awareness that is continually pushing its own boundaries, striving to take in as much as possible of the whole environment, the total situation.

There have already been efforts directed toward using gestalt awareness techniques outside the mental health professions: training workshops for doctors, dentists, educators, ministers, have been held for several years through Esalen and the various gestalt therapy institutes. There has not been, so far as I know, any sustained effort to conduct gestalt awareness training for social scientists. I do not know of any political scientist who has gone into gestalt work specifically for the purpose of developing professional skills, as Lasswell underwent training analysis in the 1930s. Nor do I know of any gestalt therapist who has systematically attempted to communicate his or her own observations and experience of political phenomena.[16]

Part of the value of gestalt as a tool for understanding political behavior is that it picks up where Maslow's work left off. Maslow gave us a theory of human needs but he left unanswered the question of why human beings so often fail to recognize their own needs, to feel them as wants, to accept them and express them in action. But it is precisely here, on the vague borderline between needs and wants, at the balancing point when a person either becomes aware of a need and deals with it or represses it by relegating it to a state of sustained unawareness, that gestalt functions.

Reich said that what political analysis should seek to explain is not why starving people steal or why exploited people strike, but why the majority of starving people do not steal and the majority of exploited people do not strike. I think this statement deserves to be taken seriously, and I think that part of the answer will be found as we develop greater awareness—of the fact that as civilized beings we have all been trained to block our own needs so that our needs are not experienced as strong and healthy wants but are instead felt, if at all, only as dull, distant, and socially respectable pain. If we can understand unawareness, we can understand political repression.

And the best place to begin in the search for such understanding—in fact probably the only place—is with oneself. The approach must be experential and not merely a different theoretical focus. The individual who has not developed a high sensitivity to his or her own needs and wants, and some ability to take care of them, is in a lamentably poor position to comprehend the needs and wants of others.

I am recommending, in short, gestalt awareness training as a part of the education of social scientists. This recommendation undoubtedly sounds a bit formidable and far-out. Perhaps I could make the same point more easily by dropping the "gestalt awareness" terminology and suggest, simply that it would be a good idea if social science education included opportunities for students to explore their own feelings as members of society—how they experience social roles, education, political processes, and so forth. Gestalt has developed a useful technology for this kind of exploration but any real recognition of the value of paying attention to one's subjective experience of political life would be a momentous step from where we are.

The academic disciplines as they stand depend heavily on the willingness of scholars and students to suppress their awareness of much that is going on in the country, in their scholastic work, and in their own bodies. Gestalt encourages one to get in touch with feelings, to become aware of authoritarianism in all its guises, to deal actively with boredom. The kind of awareness that gives one a greater ability to perceive what is going on in a courtroom or in a political meeting would also, for better or for worse, require one to take a new look at what goes on in academic conventions, department meetings, and classrooms.

Notes

[1] Frederick S. Perls, "Workshop vs. Individual Therapy," paper delivered at American Psychological Association Convention, New York City, September 1966.
[2] Paul Goodman, interview, *Psychology Today*, November 1971, p. 90.
[3] Joen Fagan and Irma Lee Shepherd, eds., *Gestalt Therapy Now* (Palo Alto, California:

Science and Behavior Books, Inc., 1970), p. 1. For more information on Perls' life see his autobiography, *In and Out the Garbage Pail* (Lafayette, Calif.: Real People Press, 1969).

[4]Quoted in Perls, *Ego, Hunger and Aggression* (San Francisco: Orbit, 1966), p. 27.

[5]Previously unpublished interview with Perls by author, 4 Jan 1968.

[6]Frederick Perls, Ralph Hefferline, and Paul Goodman, *Gestalt Therapy* (New York: Julian 1954; Delta, 1965), pp. viii–ix.

[7]Arnold R. Beisser, "The Paradoxical Theory of Change," Fagan and Shepherd, *Gestalt Therapy Now*, Harper and Row Publishers, p.77.

[8]Claudio Naranjo, "Present-Centeredness: Technique, Prescription, and Ideal," *Ibid.*, pp. 49–50.

[9]Perls, Hefferline, and Goodman, *Gestalt Therapy*, p. 215.

[10]Theodore Roszak, "Counter Culture IV: The Future as Community," *The Nation*, 206 (15 April 1968), p. 502. See also Roszak, *The Making of a Counter Culture* (New York: Doubleday Anchor, 1969).

[11]Perls, *Gestalt Therapy Verbatim* (Moab, Utah: Real People Press, 1969), pp. 16–17. Italics in original.

[12]*Ibid.*, p. 19.

[13]Perls, "Four Lectures," *Gestalt Therapy Now*, p. 16.

[14]*Gestalt Therapy Verbatim*, p. 3.

[15]Beisser, "Paradoxical Theory," p. 79.

[16]The person who came closest was Paul Goodman (see Roszak, *Making of Counter Culture*, pp. 186–204), but I personally feel that Goodman only very partially explored the possibilities of gestalt research.

VI. The Encounter Movement In Mass Society

Doesn't the form-giving greatness of leading statesmen and businessmen depend on their way of seeing the human beings with whom they have to deal not as carriers of an inexperienceable You but rather as centers of services and aspirations that have to be calculated and employed according to their specific capacities? . . . And when we turn our eyes from the leaders to the led and consider the fashion of modern work and possession, don't we find that modern developments have expunged almost every trace of a life in which human beings confront each other and have meaningful relationships?

—Martin Buber[1]

The problem of the diminished quality of interpersonal life in populous, industrialized nation-states is nothing new to political and social thought. As early as the Jacksonian era, when Alexis de Tocqueville visited the United States, he sensed a deep alienation underlying the busy lives of the citizens of the prospering young nation:

The first thing that strikes the observation is an innumerable multitude of men, all equal and alike, incessantly endeavoring to procure the petty and paltry pleasures with which they glut their lives. Each of them, living apart, is as a stranger to the fate of all the rest—his children and his private friends constitute to him the whole of mankind; as for the rest of his fellow-citizens, he is close to them, but he sees them not; he touches them, but he feels them not. . . .

Not long after Tocqueville wrote that, Karl Marx and Friedrich Engels began to mount their attack on the alienating forces of capitalism. Later Max Weber asserted that the most important and characteristic process of modern history was the "rationalization" of life, the bureaucratization of all human institutions which brought with it, in the poet Schiller's phrase, "the disenchantment of the world."

The peculiarly depersonalized nature of our society has certainly not escaped the attention of modern political science—it would be a hard thing to overlook—and indeed the study of this aspect of modern mass democracy is a fairly important occupation in the discipline. Every political scientist is familiar with such terms as alienation, depersonalization, mass society; and role theory, which is one way of dealing with the fact that people relate to one another as "centers of services and aspirations" rather than as whole human beings. Although these terms are respected items in our academic repertoire, I fear that political scientists have allowed disciplinary boundary lines to prevent them from taking notice of a movement that has arisen in *response* to the problem of alienation.

We have in our midst in America today a curious new kind of social movement, the encounter-group phenomenon. It is widely based in that it does not represent a single organization or a single ideology or a single approach; it goes by a variety of names, and as one of its leaders, Carl Rogers, has pointed out, it has found its way into an amazing range of social settings:

They [encounter groups] have operated in industries, in universities, in church settings; in government agencies, educational institutions, and penitentiaries. An astonishing range of individuals has been involved in this group experience. There have been groups for presidents of large corporations, and groups for delinquent and predelinquent adolescents. There have been groups composed of college students and faculty members, of counselors and psychotherapists; of school dropouts, of married couples, of families, including both parents and children; of confirmed drug addicts, of criminals serving sentences; of nurses, educators, teachers, school administrators, industrial managers, State Department ambassadors—even members of the Internal Revenue Service![3]

As a movement, the encounter-group thing has gotten a good deal of notice from the mass media; it has also come to the attention of most psychologists and a few sociologists—but it appears to have slipped past political scientists altogether. This fact is regrettable, because the encounter movement is also interesting politically: it represents a significant pattern of action that can hardly be ignored by political scientists who take themselves seriously as students of American culture, and it presents its own challenge to some of our commonly held values about political behavior and institutions.

Before we proceed to these things, let us take a look at the encounter movement: how it began, what it does, and what forms it takes at the present time.

Origins of the Encounter Movement

The indictment against depersonalized mass society was fairly well drawn up in the nineteenth century. I have mentioned Tocqueville, Marx and Engels, and Weber. Ferdinand Toënnies also made a valuable contribution to mass-society theory in his distinction between two kinds of social organizations—the traditional communal Gemeinschaft society and the increasingly more common Gesellschaft, the associational society to which people belong because it is a practical way of achieving a goal. The latter category of course includes most business, industry, and governmental bureaucracy; the increase of such societies results in a loss of the traditional sense of kinship, of closeness.

Existential philosophy in this century abounds with references to the problems of alienation and authenticity, with explorations into the possibility of discovering some kind of reality in the encounter with other people. Sartre, for example, wrote, "In order to get any truth about myself, I must have contact with another person. The other is indispensable to my own existence, as well as to my knowledge about myself."[4] Another recognized philosophical ancestor of the encounter movement was Martin Buber, of whose *I and Thou* (first published in 1923) Walter Kaufman recently wrote:

The aim of the book is, . . . at least in large measure, to diagnose certain tendencies in modern society—Buber speaks of "sick ages" more than forty years before it became fashionable in the West to refer to our "sick" society—and to indicate how the quality of life might be changed radically by the development of a new sense of community.[5]

J. L. Moreno, a student of existential philosophy who later developed psychodrama and several other basic encounter techniques, was already trying to start a "religion of the encounter" in Vienna in 1908; a few years later, as a young psychiatrist, he helped establish a series of personal discussion meetings among Viennese prostitutes—probably the world's first industrial encounter group.

One of the most important and productive lines of development of encounter-group work in this country began around 1947, under the inspiration of Kurt Lewin of the Massachusetts Institute of Technology. This approach has become known as sensitivity training (T-group); it initially had an *organizational* focus—the purpose was to teach interpersonal skills and the performance of roles, and to improve group communication. But as the work proceeded, many of its leaders began to feel it had a greater, and more personal, value than they had originally suspected:

For us . . . sensitivity training is no longer primarily a technique for the improvement of group functioning, the development of interpersonal skills. . . . Rather, sensitivity training is now pointed in the way of the total enhancement of the individual. Our version of sensitivity training increasingly concerns itself with the strengthening of the individual in his desire to experience people and events more fully, to know himself more intimately and accurately, to find a more significant meaning for his life.[6]

At about the same time that the T-group movement, organized as the National Training Laboratories, was getting under way, a group of people associated with Carl Rogers at the Counseling Center of the University of Chicago developed a series of intensive group experiences as a means of training personal counselors for the Veterans Administration. These groups, Rogers notes, were from the beginning "oriented primarily toward personal growth and the development and improvement of interpersonal communication and relationships, rather than having these as secondary aims."[7]

Through the 1950s Rogers was mainly concerned with the development of his client-centered approach to *individual* psychotherapy, but recently his interest has shifted to groups—with a considerable carryover of values. Rogers' approach to encounter-group work, like his approach to therapy, favors a noncontrolling and unauthoritarian form of leader-ship. The organization with which he is affiliated, the Center for Studies of the Person at La Jolla, California, became one of the many institutions offering training in the techniques of encounter-group leadership.

In the 1960s the encounter movement began another phase with the founding of the Esalen Institute at Big Sur, California. Esalen became also an important forum which brought together most of the schools of humanistic psychology, gave many psychologists their first exposure to Oriental philosophy, and encouraged the development of many new techniques of group work.[8]

Types of Encounter

The following, by no means a complete survey of encounter terminology or techniques, is intended to give the reader some familiarity with the better-known variations.

Group psychotherapy is mainly distinguishable from other forms of encounter in that the leader of the group is a licensed psychiatrist, psychologist, or counselor, while the members of the group regard themselves as "patients," "clients," or "in therapy." Any encounter-group techniques may be used by the leader; focus of group activity may be among group members or between individual members and the therapist. In gestalt work, for example, patients work as individuals with the therapist while other group members observe or function at times as a kind of "chorus" or background.

Sensitivity training and *T-group* are terms which have come into general, and varied, usage but which originally were designations for the techniques of the National Training Laboratories. The leader in these groups is usually called the "trainer" and is not expected to be a therapist, but is usually a psychologist or a person with equivalent academic background. Sensitivity training is normally conducted under the sponsorship of business corporations, churches, colleges, or other institutions.

Encounter is both a generic term for the overall movement and a description of specific types of group. Rogers and his associates often use the term *basic encounter*, usually to mean that the encounter process is relatively unstructured and, as in Roger's earlier techniques of nondirec-tional therapy, free to follow its own course. The term *open encounter* is often used to designate groups in which a variety of techniques or structures may be employed according to the preferences of the leader and the needs or demands of group members.[9] Leaders in encounter groups are usually called facilitators or simply leaders; they are normally expected to be *participants* as well; the humanistic perspective generally is suspicious of cool, uninvolved authority figures; the image of the Freudian analyst seated out of sight of the patient in a darkened room is often cited as a good example of using the professional role to avoid involving oneself in human contact. One kind of encounter is the *leaderless group*. Sometimes these grow up informally in a neighborhood or work setting where people have heard of encounter and want to try it; sometimes they are composed of individuals who have had a good deal of encounter-group experience, and often such groups are formed among encounter leaders for their own ongoing development.[10]

Psychodrama is one of the most sophisticated of encounter techniques, requiring special training for the leader, who is called a director. In this approach actual life situations are explored through spontaneous dramatizations; one member of the group, for example, may play the role of another member's spouse. "Role reversal," which offers individuals the opportunity to look at themselves from another person's perspective, is commonly employed in psychodrama.[11]

Other approaches to encounter include *sensory awakening* groups, which emphasize the development of awareness and use physical techniques including massage and exercise;[12] *attack* groups, which encourage the expression of hostility as a way of achieving interpersonal honesty (the Synanon "game" is the best known of this variety);[13] human potential groups, almost the polar opposite of attack groups, which stress the development of personal strength through affirmation from others;[14] nude encounters, an overpublicized but legitimate approach, in which the removal of clothing is encouraged as one quick way of facilitating the removal of other social barriers to communication;[15] and *marathons*, which achieve a certain kind of intensity by compressing the encounter process into a one- or two-day period, often without sleep.[16]

In general, the timing of encounter-group experience varies from the *ongoing group*, which meets on a regular basis (such as once a week) for a period extending from a few weeks indefinitely, to the *workshop*, which meets once for a day, a weekend, a one-week or a longer session. Some ongoing groups periodically schedule workshops or marathons as a supplement to regular meetings.

Another important distinction is made between "imbedded" groups, which are in or relevant to the ongoing social environment—work, family, etc.—of its members, and groups which take the individual away from his or her normal environment.[17]

What Happens in Encounter

The experiences vary enormously, of course, depending on the personality and ability of leader, composition of group, techniques employed, and time and place. But certain hypotheses are applicable to all encounter experiences. The following summary by Rogers fairly well outlines the common expectations:

> A facilitator can develop, in a group which meets intensively, a psychological climate of safety in which freedom of expression and reduction of defensiveness gradually occur.

In such a psychological climate many of the immediate feeling reactions of each member toward others, and of each member toward himself, tend to be expressed.

A climate of mutual trust develops out of this mutual freedom to express real feelings, positive and negative. Each member moves toward greater acceptance of his total being—emotional, intellectual, and physical—as it *is*, including its potential.

With individuals less inhibited by defensive rigidity, the possibility of change in personal attitudes and behavior, in professional methods, in administrative procedures and relationships, becomes less threatening.

With the reduction of defensive rigidity, individuals can hear each other, can learn from each other, to a greater extent.

There is a development of feedback from one person to another, such that each individual learns how he appears to others and what impact he has in interpersonal relationships.

With this greater freedom and improved communication, new ideas, new concepts, new directions emerge. Innovation can become a desirable rather than a threatening possibility.

These learnings in the group experience tend to carry over, temporarily or more permanently, into the relationships with spouse, children, students, subordinates, peers, and even superiors following the group experience.[18]

There seems to be general consensus that the above processes do, in varying degrees, take place in groups.[19] But there is still plenty of controversy over the real value of the encounter experience. Many people doubt its carryover potency, especially for those who attend a weekend workshop and then return to face alone the unchanged coldness of their jobs and home lives. Many professional psychotherapists fear the danger of possible psychic damage to individuals who venture into highly emotional territory without the guidance and protection of trained experts, i.e., professional psychotherapists.

Checklist for Group Leaders[20]

Leader moves away from:	Leader moves toward:
1. Being impersonal, "in role"	1. Being personal, non-role
2. Selecting my behaviors because they are helpful or therapeutic (a role prescription)	2. Responding to my current feelings and perceptions (showing my self)
3. Focus upon relations between role and role (leader and member; member and member)	3. Focus upon relations between persons and persons
4. Responding to what patients or members seem to need (programming)	4. Responding to how I see and feel about my relationships now (being spontaneous)
5. Screening my responses and modeling appropriate, relevant, helpful, role, or professional aspects of self	5. Minimal screening but sharing all areas of self, however relevant or professional they may seem to me to be

6. Responding to the other as a client, patient, member, or person needing help	6. Responding to the other as a unique person, *qua* person
7. Concern for changing, curing, or remedying the deficient individual	7. Concern for growth and development of each of us in all of our relationships
8. Being consistent with my theory of action, training, therapy or group growth	8. Focus upon intuition, "gut feel" of what to do: following impulse
9. Focus upon motives, interpretations, and other derivative, inferential, or role concepts	9. Focus upon more available, direct, experienced and visible behavior
10. Focus upon separate, autonomous individuals or entities, as entities	10. Focus on *relationships* (on how it is now between or among us)
11. Focus on abstraction, generality, or principle	11. Focus on concrete, primitive and elemental feelings and perceptions
12. Focus upon evaluative or moral judgments	12. Focus on descriptive statements about feelings and perceptions
13. Focus on and concern for *then* (other relationships in the past or future and on the past history of members)	13. Focus on and concern for *now* (how each of us feels and sees things at this moment)
14. Focus on and concern for *there* (data from other relationships and contexts)	14. Focus on and concern for *here* (feelings and perceptions visible and available to all)
15. Focus upon description of the passive self as a static being	15. Focus upon description of the dynamic, inprocess, becoming organism/person
16. Focus upon limitations of the person	16. Focus upon strengths and growing edges of the person
17. Focus upon punishment and rewards	17. Focus upon flowing behaviors and feelings
18. Focus upon legality, "contracts," norms, controls	18. Focus upon flow, fluidity of temporary, self-sustaining systems
19. Focus upon the terminology of fear, risk, caution, and conservation	19. Focus upon trust, venture, impulse, and liberation
20. Focus upon words, semantics, and speech	20. Focus upon non-verbal and body flow and organic integration

Much of the criticism of the encounter-group movement carries a political tone. There has been powerful conservative opposition to sensitivity-training programs in public school systems in many parts of the country. Several years ago an article in *American Opinion*, the journal of the John Birch Society, warned that sensitivity training was a form of "brainwashing" being foisted upon unsuspecting Americans by "the usual forces of the conspiratorial left."[21] More recently a psychiatrist described the encounter movement, particularly Esalen, as a part of the "quest of the counterculture," aimed at "an exorcism of the superego," a group assault on "many of the sanctions which modern society has deemed essential to a civilized community."[22] The movement has also been attacked from the left by some radical activists; they regard encounter as an insidious process which can divert the revolutionary from the true goal, dissolve his or her ardor in a warm bath of instant friendship.

How Political Objectives Grow Out of Encounter Groups

In my opinion the encounter movement can be understood as a challenge to the dehumanized, alienated quality of life in a modern mass society. It is especially relevant to those whose lives are centered in the Gesellschaft, the massive depersonalized organization whose primary purpose is the realization of some external goal—be it the production of cars or the selling of insurance or the collection of taxes—and not the satisfaction of the emotional needs of its members. Whether individuals come into "imbedded" groups which are created within the organization or go off somewhere to join an ongoing group or a workshop is, from this point of view, quite irrelevant. They are searching for something which the society does not otherwise provide. Most people, of course, approach the encounter-group movement as part of a personal search— they sense the absence of spontaneity, honesty, openness and closeness to others in their own lives, and are trying to do something about it. For others the movement is more political: it is seen as an organized assault upon some of the greatest failings of American society. Encounter-group values become the basis for a critique of the values that currently govern the way our institutions are structured and the ways people relate to one another in public life. Let us look more closely at this transformation of encounter-group goals into political objectives.

I have mentioned the value of *spontaneity*. J. L. Moreno, one of the earliest pioneers of the encounter movement, feels that the characteristic malaise of modern human beings is a pathological loss of spontaneity. He believes that losing spontaneity means not only a loss of personal effectiveness (spontaneity is defined as the ability to deal in a new way with a familiar situation, or in an adequate way with a new one), but also a loss of creativity and even a loss of a certain regulating principle in social situations. He says, "*It is spontaneity which produces order*, not the laws which are themselves an artefact of a spontaneous order."[23]

Recently Lewis Yablonsky has expanded some of Moreno's ideas into a charge that American society is suffering from a loss of spontaneity on a massive scale, to the point of a social pathology:

Modern mass society, the technocratic state, and their machine domination of people have grossly altered the patterns and styles of human interaction. Their ultimate impact has been the dehumanization of people to the point where much of their social interaction is machine-like. People's emotions, spontaneity, creativity, personal identity, and ability to be compassionate are increasingly reduced to a set of robopathic responses. This subtle social pathology infects all levels of human interaction, from interpersonal relationships in a primary group, such as family or love relationships, on through secondary groups, such as corporate and political associations. I am alleging, therefore, that technocracies and the machine way of life have transformed *human groups* partially and in some cases completely into *social machines*. A social machine is a dehumanized interaction system wherein people's relationships are relatively devoid of sincere emotions, creativity, and compassion.[24]

Yablonsky coins the term *robopath* to describe individuals who exhibit the symptoms of this social malaise: ritualism, past-orientation, self-righteousness, and alienation.[25] Also he charges that robopathology is not merely the special sickness of the faceless masses but is equally—if not more—evident among its powerful leaders. In fact he offers up the governor of California as a living example of what he means by an image-oriented robopath.[26]

As with spontaneity, *honesty* is seen as a particularly essential quality of interpersonal relationships, whose absence will be felt as painful for individuals. Sidney Jourard has written of this:

We conceal and camouflage our true being before others to foster a sense of safety, to protect ourselves against unwanted but expected criticism, hurt, or rejection. The protection is purchased at a steep price. When we are not truly known by the other people in our lives, we are misunderstood. When we are not known, even by family and friends, we join the all too numerous "lonely crowd." Worse, when we succeed too well in hiding our being from others, we tend to lose touch with our real selves, and this loss of self contributes to illness in its myriad forms.

The curious thing to me, as a psychologist, is that we have not seriously questioned man's *decision* to hide rather than to reveal himself. Indeed, self-concealment is regarded as the most natural state for grown men.[27]

The development of a personal capacity for honesty and openness with others becomes the goal of encounter-group participation. This, too, is becoming a political objective. Consider William Schutz's discussion of honesty and openness in a political frame of reference:

The honesty revolution of which encounter groups are a central part is a revolution against the fabric of our society. It has become very much a part of human life to be devious and hypocritical and the youth and black revolts center around this issue. In my view this is a revolt too long in coming. . . .

Hypocrisy is widely accepted and assumed to be the preferred way to live. Former Secretary of State Dean Rusk was once quoted in *Time*: "I feel that diplomacy requires calm. Diplomacy has worked for hundreds of years to eliminate the accidents of personality from the conduct of State affairs. That's why, for example, we sign a diplomatic note, 'Accept, Excellency, the assurances of my highest consideration,' when in fact, you're telling him to go to Hell."

I find this a revealing statement. First, a person as highly placed as the Secretary of State approves of lying as a characteristic mode of relating. Second, he naively assumes that it is possible to eliminate personality from diplomatic negotiations. Third, he assumes that conventional diplomacy has worked for all these years, although one of its primary goals, peace, has virtually never been achieved. . . . [28]

There are a couple of things about this particular kind of social criticism which deserve our attention. One is that it is quite deliberately and consciously *ad hominem*. It does not talk about policies or political offices in the abstract but about specific people and the way they act toward others; personal life style, the presence or absence of such qualities as openness and spontaneity, are not peripheral to the issue— they *are* the issue. It is not unusual for political discussion to focus on personality, but it has traditionally centered on such characteristics as "leadership ability" or a more abstract form of honesty; this concern with personal openness, this suspicion that there is something quite dangerous about the guarded, uptight politician is, I think, a subtle indicator of an important shift in the quality of political dialogue.

The other thing that I wish to point out about this kind of criticism is that it springs from the conviction that alternative styles of behavior are both available and practical. The basis of the conviction is not idealistic—that people should behave differently toward each other—but experiential—that people can and do behave differently toward each other and it works. I have quoted Yablonsky, a sociologist, and Schutz, a psychologist, each of whom has about twenty years of experience with encounter groups, and has seen thousands of people learn to function effectively in a somewhat more open fashion.

As we focus on the two characteristics I have mentioned—the determination to make personal openness a political issue, the conviction that alternative styles of interpersonal relationship are truly available—we begin to get a sense of the unique political challenge that the encounter movement presents, the unique crusade that it is trying to mobilize. It is nothing less than an attempt to transform the whole society's style of interpersonal relating. Like gestalt therapy (with which it overlaps) it aims not at the institutional superstructure but at the person-to-person foundation of society.

I have discussed the movement both as a personal search for different and more satisfactory ways of being and relating and as a political movement aimed at bringing about a basic transformation in the rules of the game. We should also remember that it is an *intellectual* movement. It brings together the efforts of a growing number of psychologists, sociologists, educators, and specialists in organization and communications who take seriously the fundamental human needs for affection and belongingness, the value of openness and spontaneity; these social scientists are working on the task of formulating a theory based on these needs and values so that the techniques of interpersonal action and the styles of institutional structure may be developed to produce satisfaction of these needs on a massive scale.

This task is obviously an enormous one, related to the main themes of modern history. It is a response to the disruptions of the quality of human life which have resulted from the Industrial Revolution, urbanization, population growth—the emergence of mass society. Its goal is to move forward into the highly technological interrelated world society that appears to be our inevitable future, while creating in a new and appropriate form something that can best be described, in terms of our past historical experience of it, as a sense of community.

Notes

[1] Buber, *I and Thou*, translation by Walter Kaufman. Copyright © 1970 Charles Scribner's Sons.

[2] Alexis de Tocqueville, *Democracy in America*, trans. Henry Reeve (London: Longmans, Green, and Co., 1889), 2:290.

[3] *Carl Rogers on Encounter Groups* (New York: Harper and Row, 1970), p. 2.

[4] Jean-Paul Sartre, *Existentialism* (New York: Philosophical Library, 1947), p. 44.

[5] Walter Kaufman, Introduction to *I and Thou*, p. 38.

[6] I. Wechsler, F. Massarik, and R. Tannenbaum, "The Self in Process: A Sensitivity Training Emphasis," in *Issues in Human Relations Training* eds., I. Wechsler and E. Schein (Washington, D.C.; NTL Selected Readings Series, No. 5, 1962).

[7] *Rogers on Encounter Groups*, p. 4.

[8] A good introduction to Esalen encounter work can be found in the publications of Esalen training director William Schutz—*Joy* (New York: Grove, 1967) and *Here Comes Everybody* (New York: Harper and Row, 1971). A good autobiographical account of life at Esalen is Stuart Miller, *Hot Springs: The True Adventures of the First New York Jewish Literary Intellectual in the Human Potential Movement* (New York: Viking, 1972).

[9] One survey of such techniques is in *Here Comes Everybody*, pp. 126–202.

[10] Rogers (*On Encounter Groups*, p. 119) believes that leaderless groups can be effective, even superior to groups with leaders.

[11] A brief introduction to psychodrama is Robert W. Siroka, Ellen K. Siroka and Gilbert A. Schloss, *Sensitivity Training and Group Encounter* (New York: Grosset & Dunlap, 1971), pp. 103–127.

[12] Bernard Gunther, *Sense Relaxation: Below Your Mind* (New York: Macmillan, 1968) and *What To Do Till the Messiah Comes* (New York: Macmillan, 1971).

[13] Lewis Yablonsky, *Synanon: The Tunnel Back* (Baltimore: Penguin, 1967).

[14] Herbert A. Otto, *Group Methods to Actualize Human Potential* (La Jolla, California: National Center for the Exploration of Human Potential, 1970).

[15] Paul A. Bindrim, "A Report on a Nude Marathon," in Siroka et al., *Sensitivity Training*, pp. 149–163.

[16] Siroka et al., pp. 131–164.

[17] Rogers, *On Encounter Groups*, p. 119.

[18] Rogers, *On Encounter Groups*, pp. 6–7.

[19] Research on encounter is surveyed in Jack Gibb, "The Effects of Human Relations Training," in *Handbook of Psychotherapy and Behavior Change* eds. A. E. Bergin and S. L. Garfield (New York: Wiley, 1970), pp. 2114–76.

[20] Jack R. Gibb, *TORI Theory and Practice*, in J. W. Pfeiffer and John E. Jones (eds.) *The 1972 Annual Handbook For Group Facilitators* University Associates, P. O. Box 615 Iowa City, Iowa, 52240. p. 159.

[21] Gary Allen, "Hate Therapy," *American Opinion*, January 1968, pp. 73–86.

[22] Alan A. Stone, "The Quest of the Counterculture," *International Journal of Psychiatry*, 1972, 9:248.

[23] J. L. Moreno, *Psychodrama*, vol. 1 (New York: Beacon House, 1946), p. 9.

[24] Lewis Yablonsky, *Robopaths* (Indianapolis: Bobbs-Merrill, 1972), pp. 91–92.

[25] *Ibid.*, p. 7.

[26] *Ibid.*, p. 24.

[27] From *The Transparent Self* by Sidney M. Jourard. © 1971, 1964 by Litton Educational Publishing, Inc. Reprinted by permission of Van Nostrand Reinhold Company.

[28] William Schutz, *Here Comes Everybody*, (New York: Harper and Row 1971) p. 31.

VII. The Politics Of Satori

The whole difficulty of both psychotherapy and liberation is that the problems which they address lie in the social institutions in whose terms we think and act.
  —Alan Watts[1]

Anyone who wants to become familiar with humanistic psychology needs to be aware of the fact that an important source of philosophical influence in the movement comes from outside Western culture, from the Orient. Many concepts, values, and techniques of Eastern systems such as Zen, Yoga, and Sufism have found their way into psychological theory, therapy, and encounter-group practice. Recently there has been a considerable amount of laboratory work by experimental psychologists in such fields as the EEG (electroencephalogram) measurement of the mental states achieved in meditation and the various kinds of physical control—heartbeat, temperature, respiration, etc.—practiced by Yoga masters.[2]

I will try to introduce the reader to some characteristic ideas of Oriental thought in this chapter, and to show how they relate to humanistic psychology generally and to the perspective on the individual and culture that is the main theme of this book. I will not pretend to "survey" these systems; I am not an expert on them; if I were, it would still not be possible to survey in a chapter several centuries of work and teaching in a number of widely different cultures. I will deal here only with the philosophy of Zen and will rely mainly on interpretations of it by Western writers.

To begin with, it would be valuable to avoid thinking of Zen as a religion in the Western sense. There is scarcely any mention of a diety in it; rather—like Yoga, Sufism and various other Eastern disciplines—it is primarily a technique for the development of consciousness. Realizing this, we can more easily understand why it is of interest to psychologists, and particularly to psychologists whose orientation is more toward the continuation of human growth than toward therapy as it has usually been understood.

When we deal with Zen as a psychological system we come again to the concept of internalization of social norms. We have already encountered the idea, in Freudian theory and again in gestalt therapy, that all people incorporate some of the rules of society into their own psyches as conscience or superego. Zen goes a long step further and asserts that all perceptions of reality, even the very sense of self, are products of social conditioning. This idea, too, is not entirely alien to Western thought. Such writers as George Herbert Mead and Charles H. Cooley have argued that the "self" of every individual is a concept developed out of social interaction with others,[3] the symbolic interactionist school of sociology holds that most of what we call "thinking"—the ways we interpret and organize sense perceptions, our most basic concepts of "reality"—are shaped and limited by the culture's symbolic systems, especially its language.[4] This idea is also found in modern linguistic analysis, and in general semantics.

Erich Fromm describes the cultural conditioning of the individual consciousness this way:

> Human awareness is organized in various possible ways, and for any experience to come into awareness, it must be comprehensible in the categories in which conscious thought is organized. Some of the categories, such as time and space, may be universal, and may constitute categories of perception common to all men. Others, such as causality, may be a valid category for many, but not for all, forms of conscious human perception. Other categories are even less general and differ from culture to culture. However this may be, experience can enter into awareness only under the condition that it can be perceived, related, and ordered in terms of a conceptual system and of its categories. This system is in itself a result of social evolution. Every society, by its own practice of living and by the mode of relatedness, of feeling, and perceiving, develops a system of categories which determines the forms of awareness. This system works, as it were, like a *socially conditioned filter*; experience cannot enter awareness unless it can penetrate this filter.[5]

The Social Relevance of Zen

If we grant, with Fromm and the symbolic interactionists, that this kind of a conditioning process does take place, then we can work toward an understanding of the social relevance of Zen by asking three questions: (1) What does this conditioning do to the individual? (2) Is it possible to become deconditioned, to throw away the social filter? (3) What are the larger political implications of such a process?

(1) Functions of Conditioning for the Individual

There is a general consensus among psychologists of all persuasions that such social learning processes as the acquisition of language are absolutely necessary to the development of cognitive ability, and that it is scarcely possible to conceive of a human being except as an organism that has developed such abilities.

In daily life, this conditioning provides the individual with security, identity, and a means of communication. One has one's name, one's personal and cultural history, one's roles, one's view of the world and the universe, one's social values and tastes. All these things provide a certain stability, enable men and women to move through life with some sense of knowing who they are and what they are doing—perhaps most important of all, provide a sense of belongingness, because socially recognized values and perceptions can be shared with others.

But still this shared reality is a *social reality*, and it may create problems as well as solve them. Alan Watts, one of the best-known Western interpreters of Zen thought, says:

There is direct conflict between what the individual organism is and what others say it is and expect it to be. The rules of social communication often contain contradictions which lead to impossible dilemmas in thought, feeling, and action. Or it may be that confusion of oneself with a limiting and impoverished view of one's role or identity creates feelings of isolation, loneliness, and alienation.[6]

It seems strange, on the face of it, that Watts should use the word *alienation*—which of course means a state of being cut off, estranged—precisely when he is describing the things people do to *belong*, the roles and identities they adopt as *members* of society. Yet that is clearly what he means. Fromm uses the same word, and uses it to describe a massive cultural crisis in which alienation is a characteristic experience:

While the majority of people living in the West do not consciously feel as if they were living through a crisis of Western culture (probably never have the majority of people in a radically critical situation been aware of the crisis), there is agreement, at least among a number of critical observers, as to the existence and the nature of this crisis. It is the crisis which has been described as "malaise," "ennui," "Mal du siecle," the deadening of life, the automatization of man, his alienation from himself, from his fellow man and from nature.[7]

At another point Fromm says, "The content of consciousness is mostly fictional and delusional, and precisely does not represent reality. . . . Most of what is in our consciousness is 'false consciousness' and . . . it is essentially society that fills us with these fictitious and unreal notions."[8] Watts says simply: "The rules of communication are not necessarily the rules of the universe. . . . "[9]

Now, what both of these writers are asserting is that the socially conditioned consciousness is not only a survival mechanism, but also a kind of psychological straitjacket that, in the very process of giving men and women a place in the social order, cuts them off from something else. Careful footnote-watchers will already have noticed that both of the discussions from which I have been quoting are about the relationship between Zen and psychotherapy; they are both investigations of Zen as medicine for the socially conditioned mind, a way of piercing the social filter and seeing the world with new eyes. Many readers will also have detected a similarity to gestalt therapy, with its belief in a deeper, more natural ordering principle that can successfully take over and guide the life of the person who has become free from the internalized authority of society. This point is one of many at which Zen comes close to humanistic psychology.

(2) Zen as a Deconditioning Process

Zen is a training process aimed at a specific goal, the *satori* experience. In this discussion I am going to reverse the order of things—talk about the goal first and then about the approach to it.

Equivalent terms for satori in English are enlightenment, awakening, liberation; in Zen teaching, satori is a single, instantaneous breakthrough, a sudden comprehension of the truth. Accounts of satori vary tremendously, but it always comes across in the literature as a powerful experience:

In many cases it seemed as though the bottom had fallen out of the universe, as though the oppressiveness of the outer world had suddenly melted like a vast mountain of ice, for Satori is release from one's habitual state of tenseness, of clinging to false ideas of possession. The whole rigid structure which is man's interpretation of life suddenly drops to pieces, resulting in a sense of boundless freedom. . . . [10]

Another thing that emerges quite clearly from the various descriptions of satori is that it is not a trance or hallucinatory state. It may be accompanied by a certain vividness of sensory experience ("The spring flower will look prettier, and the mountain stream runs cooler and more transparent"[11]), but it should not be confused with the states of consciousness achieved through drug use or through some of the more advanced yoga practices.[12] "Zen," one Japanese teacher wrote, "is your everyday mind."

Although the satori experience is the desired end of Zen training, it is not a *guaranteed* end, nor is its timing in any way predictable. The Zen literature is full of accounts of students who attain satori almost immediately, and it is generally conceded that enlightenment may be attained by an individual without any training whatever. On the other hand it is possible to study for years without achieving enlightenment.

There are two basic tools in the Zen technique: meditation and the use of *koan*.

Nobody knows precisely what happens in Zen meditation practice, but a few points about it are quite clear and relevant to this discussion. It is not cognitive or devotional as are various Christian traditions which use meditation as a form of prayer or as a means of concentrating upon some principle or aspect of God. Zen meditation *is*, however, an intense form of concentration: nonverbal concentration. The various meditation techniques—counting of breath, etc.—all involve a deliberate cessation of the "internal monologue," of discursive verbal thinking; this cessation is particularly important if we accept the argument that language is the main vehicle of socially conditioned thinking. The verbalizing, describing state of mind in which all experience is appraised, categorized, understood, related to previous experience, is precisely the opposite of the empty, open, directly perceiving state of mind prized by the Zen tradition. The desired condition of Zen meditation, then, is one of relaxed, awake attentiveness.

This kind of meditation—thanks to a certain amount of faddishness, a good deal of excellent research, and the acceptance by many clinicians of its value as a kind of mental exercise—is no longer entirely exotic to Westerners. The koan, however, remain inscrutable. What sense are even the most open-minded of us to make out of such phrases as these?

The sound of one hand clapping,

or:

Thinking neither of good nor evil, tell me
at this moment what was your original aspect
before your mother and father were born?

Such koan as the above are, especially in the Rinzai school of Zen, a central element of training and practice.[13] They are taken with great seriousness, and many of them have been in use for centuries. Yet they seem to be nothing more than examples of a particularly irritating kind of Oriental coyness, a cultivation of meaninglessness for its own sake. However, I think that we need to consider them in the light of the main themes of this chapter—that Zen is essentially a deconditioning process which helps people to see through their own socially formed consciousness and that language gives the form and structure to that social consciousness. Then we can begin to understand, if not the koan themselves, at least the general reason for their use. They attack language, they attack the cultural logical systems upon which language is built.[14] The koan, given to students to work with, annoy and baffle them until the effort drives them through the impasse into a state of mind in which they perceive clearly, *on their own*, that langage and logic are merely symbols of reality, which human consciousness may use but does not have to be bound by. One authority on the koan says:

> The koan is not a conundrum to be solved by a nimble wit. It is not a verbal psychiatric device for shocking the disintegrated ego of a student into some kind of stability. Nor, in my opinion, is it ever a paradoxical statement except to those who view it from the outside. When the koan is resolved it is realized to be a simple and clear statement made from the state of consciousness which it has helped to awaken.[15]

It is interesting, in view of the above assertion, that koan are used not only as a way of attaining satori, but are employed at times by Zen masters to test the degree of liberation of students who think they *have* attained satori.[16]

(3) The Political Meaning of Zen Enlightenment

The two main writers that I have been using as sources in this chapter, Fromm and Watts, both believe that Zen liberation is essentially a release from the psychological conditioning of the society. This release does not preclude valuing the *satori* as a profound spiritual experience; one cannot easily ignore the virtual unanimity, among those who have reported such experiences that they are attended by a feeling of spiritual peace. But when we realize satori brings liberation, we have a new and productive understanding of a mysticism which to many people seems to be totally meaningless. Fromm, for example, is quite explicit in his opinion that the social conditioning of the intellect is closely related to political domination:

Most of what people have in their conscious minds is fiction and delusion; this is the case not so much because people would be *incapable* of seeing the truth as because of the function of society. Most of human history (with the exception of some primitive societies) is characterized by the fact that a small minority has ruled over and exploited the majority of its fellows. In order to do so, the minority has usually used force; but force is not enough. In the long run, the majority has had to accept its own exploitation voluntarily—and this is only possible if its mind has been filled with all sorts of lies and fictions, justifying and explaining its acceptance of the minority's rule. However, this is not the only reason for the fact that most of what people have in their awareness about themselves, others, society, etc., is fiction. In its historical development each society becomes caught in its own need to survive in the particular form in which it has developed, and it usually accomplishes this survival by ignoring the wider human aims which are common to all men. This contradiction between the social and the universal aim leads also to the fabrication (on a social scale) of all sorts of fictions and illusions which have the function to deny and to rationalize the dichotomy between the goals of humanity and the goals of a given society.[17]

If this is true, then obviously an awakening from the socially conditioned consciousness is an experience that profoundly transforms one's relationship to the political order, and the word *liberation* as a synonym for satori takes on a political meaning. The individual so liberated is still subject to the laws of the state, of course, but the state's roots in consciousness have virtually disappeared. And we know that it is consciousness—shared cultural values, socialization, role behavior, the social sense of identity—which holds political orders together, not laws and force. Yet Watts says: "Liberation is not revolution. It is not going out of one's way to disturb the social order by casting doubt upon the conventional ideas by which people hold together." One reason that the Zen way of liberation is not political revolution is that it is in no way a mass movement; nobody has found a way to bring about enlightenment en masse by manifesto, demonstration, or propaganda. The experience cannot be simply given, even to a single person:

The whole technique of liberation requires that the individual shall find out the truth for himself. Simply to tell it is not convincing. Instead, he must be asked to experiment, to act consistently upon assumptions which he holds to be true until he finds out otherwise.[18]

Even with this inherent limitation upon the capacity of Zen masters to help great numbers of people break through the social conditioning of consciousness, it is surprising that Zen is hardly ever accused of endangering any culture, Eastern or Western. Watts sees this as an impressive evidence of the cleverness of its leaders; "The Eastern ways of liberation have been astonishingly ingenious; their masters, whom society would have felt to be utterly subversive, have convinced society that they are its very pillars."[19]

If we are to take Zen at all seriously, then I think we can see that it does provide an important and radically different perspective on some of the key concepts of traditional political philosophy—obligation, authority, etc.—and on some of the subjects of current behavioral research, especially socialization. To look at the political order as in a sense resting upon the collective consciousness of a number of individuals—a largely false consciousness at that—is to call into question many of the familiar ideas about the relationship between the individual psyche, the society, and the culture. To put the matter in a cherished old academic phraseology: if Alan Watts is more than half right, then Talcott Parsons is more than half wrong.

Zen also sheds some light on an assertion which is most important to political theory and which is being advanced vociferously these days by a number of radical psychologists. This assertion, basically, is that the prevailing political order enforces not only certain patterns of economic and social interaction but also a fundamental definition of reality, a world view and value system which is the basis for all power, and which is defined not simply as patriotism but as sanity. In the works of Laing and Szasz, for example, we find a kind of psychological pluralism which is far broader than conventional political pluralism; it recognizes not only differing value systems and interests but totally differing worlds, differing consciousnesses, differing realities.

This brings us back to my basic argument that humanistic psychology can best be understood historically as a response to cultural change; in all its variations it reveals a search for some kind of common transcultural meeting ground where human beings can recognize one another and communicate. In this context Zen, which teaches that all people contain within themselves a true and unconditioned consciousness which can be trained to break through and make contact with its environment, offers an important contribution. The question we should consider now is whether that contribution can be dealt with at all in the social sciences, in view of its difficulty and apparent lack of logic.

To get at this question let me first of all confront squarely its difficulty—and Zen *is* difficult. Here, in a short brutal summation, is what it says:

1. The normal state of mind is largely delusional, a kind of waking dream, the product of social conditioning.
2. An awakening from that state of mind is possible; the awakened state is a new way of existing in precisely the same perceptual world, not a trance or hallucination.
3. The awakened state can never be accurately preconceived by the person who has not attained it.
4. Although guidance in achieving the awakened state is possible, the state cannot be simply "taught"; individuals must ultimately discover it for themselves.
5. When the state is achieved, it is not communicable to those who have not achieved it; it cannot be verbally described.

This idea of the incommunicability of states of consciousness is new to the social sciences but not to psychotherapy; indeed, a characteristic plight of therapists is one of *knowing and seeing* certain things about what patients are doing, and trying to find some way to get them to discover those things for themselves. Herbert Fingarette, another writer who has investigated the parallels between Zen and psychotherapy, writes:

Most often the anxiety-motivation of behavior is masked, the behavior frequently being rationalized. Thus the man who has always worked compulsively at his job is likely to be unable to distinguish his behavior from that of industrious and enthusiastic but anxiety-free work. The attempts of others to use language to suggest to him the subtle but profound difference in the "feel" of the two experiences will most likely be met by him either with incomprehension or derisive scorn, or both. When he asks them to describe in "plain" language how *they* approach their work, victory is his—for they have to use the very same language-forms he does. If someone says that anxiety-free work has a kind of absorbed and devoted character, the compulsive replies that those are just the words that describe his work! And he is right.[20]

Experimental psychology has found it quite easy to deal with Zen, in a limited way. One of its most common "languages"—the measurement of human brain waves by the electroencephalogram—is used to communicate some clearly perceived data about Zen meditators. This does not mean, of course, that the symbolic systems available to the experimental psychologists can "understand" Zen fully, but at least they make it possible to know for sure that something is there, that different states of consciousness do exist, even though the subjective content of such states remains elusive.

The social sciences at this stage have a greater difficulty, but I think it can be remedied as we begin to adopt a more sophisticated view of science. Theorists in the physical sciences—ironically, the field that social scientists have tried hardest to imitate—make room for new concepts with relative ease. In dealing with things not fully understood they sometimes formulate descriptive terms—wavicle, antimatter, quasar—which are tentative, exploratory, and hypothetical, meant to be used when they are useful and in time superseded. In the social sciences, however, the pursuit of what is thought to be proper scientific rigor demands that all things be precisely and unambiguously defined; the unspoken assumption which lurks behind this demand is that everything that cannot be so defined does not exist.

It is, I believe, entirely consonant with good scientific practice to deal with the idea of alternate states of consciousness in a tentative way and, without either rejecting it forthwith or swallowing it whole, see if it opens up any new vistas in our understanding of politics and society. To do so would be to admit the possibility that the human mind is as vast in complexity, and still as imperfectly understood, as the atoms and the galaxies. To refuse to do so would be like insisting the world is flat because it is too much trouble to redraw the maps.

Notes

[1]Alan Watts, *Psychotherapy East and West* (New York: Random House, Inc. and Pantheon Books, a division of Random House, Inc. 1961) p. 39.
[2]Charles T. Tart, ed., *Altered States of Consciousness* (New York: Wiley, 1969), pp. 485–517.

[3]Several viewpoints on this issue are represented in Chad Gordon and Kenneth J. Gergen, eds., *The Self in Social Interaction* (New York: Wiley, 1968).

[4]Alfred R. Lindesmith and Anselm L. Strauss, *Social Psychology* (New York: Holt, Rinehart and Winston, 1968), pp. 233–254.

[5]Erich Fromm, with D. T. Suzuki and Richard De Martino, *Zen Buddhism and Psychoanalysis* (New York: Harper Colophon, 1970), p. 99. Italics in original.

[6]*Psychotherapy East and West*, p. 16.

[7]Fromm, *Zen and Psychoanalysis*, pp. 78–79.

[8]*Ibid.*, p. 98.

[9]Watts, *Psychotherapy*, p. 15.

[10]Watts, *The Spirit of Zen* Reprinted by permission of Grove Press, Inc. Copyright © 1958 by Alan B. Watts.

[11]D. T. Suzuki, *Introduction to Zen Buddhism* (London: Rider, 1949), p. 97.

[12]Tart, *Altered Consciousness*, p. 486. The laboratory research shows a considerable difference between Zen and Yoga adepts in EEG patterns and response to sensory stimuli, which appears to be consistent with the goals of the two disciplines.

[13]As a general introduction to the Rinzai school I recommend Philip Kapleau, *Three Pillars of Zen* (Boston: Beacon Press, 1967).

[14]From the standpoint of Western culture we can best describe this logical heritage in terms of the Aristotelian dualities. Zen was mainly developed in China, in a culture pervaded by Confucian logic. See D. T. Suzuki, *Zen Buddhism* (New York: Doubleday Anchor, 1956), pp. 27–80.

[15]Ruth Fuller Sasaki, with Isshu Miura, *The Zen Koan* (New York: Harcourt, Brace Jovanovich, Inc. 1965), pp. xi–xii.

[16]*The Spirit of Zen*, p. 69.

[17]Fromm, *Zen and Psychoanalysis*, pp. 97–98.

[18]*Psychotherapy East and West*, p. 50.

[19]*Ibid.*, p. 51.

[20]Herbert Fingarette, "The Ego and Mystic Selflessness," Reprinted from *Psychoanalysis and the Psychoanalytic Review.* Vol. 45, No. 1, 1958 through the courtesy of the Editors and the Publisher, National Psychological Association for Psychoanalysis, New York, N.Y.

VIII. The Evolutionary Perspective

The primacy of mathematical physics as the science of sciences, as the exemplary core of general scientific progress, which it has been since the seventeenth century, is now passing. The new hub is that of the life sciences, of the lines of inquiry that lead outward from biology, molecular chemistry, biochemistry, biogenetics, and ethology in its largest sense. These lines now seem to radiate and spiral toward every quarter of scientific and philosophic pursuits, as did the physics of Descartes and Newton.

—George Steiner[1]

We are familiar now with the idea that one can "know" something abstractly or theoretically and still hardly know it at all, not have assimilated it into full awareness. With that in mind, I want to begin this chapter by listing a few propositions which I believe nearly all of us would readily grant to be obvious and true:

1. The human race represents a stage in a long evolutionary development which has produced intelligent life on Earth and which is still in progress.
2. There is intelligence in the universe, as evidenced by the fact that we are a part of the universe and possess intelligence.
3. Our intelligence has now reached the point, in science and technology, at which we are beginning to be capable of making decisions that will influence future evolution.

None of the above is particularly controversial, yet if they are taken together and consciously applied to the things we think about, as citizens and social scientists, they form a whole new perspectiv: a fundamentally different way of looking at human beings and political organizations.

To understand that this evolutionary, biological perspective I am talking about is truly different from other approaches, let us take another look at the philosophical underpinnings of behavioral political science. Most behavioralists date their revolution from the postwar years when their new scientific viewpoint and values impressed themselves so persuasively upon so many young political scientists. But there had been another scientific revolution in political science a few decades earlier that had not been so successful,[2] and there had been yet another two centuries before when the discoveries of Isaac Newton became known to the world. One historian's account of this scientist's impact goes:

Newton struck the imagination of this time . . . just because his important conclusions were arrived at by such commonplace methods. If the character of so intangible a thing as light could be discovered by playing with a prism, if, by looking through a telescope and doing a sum in mathematics, the force which held the planets could be identified with the force that made an apple fall to the ground, there seemed to be no end to what might be definitely known about the universe. . . . Newton, more than any man before him, so it seemed to the eighteenth century, banished mystery from the world. In his hands "Philosophy" came to be no more than a matter of observation and mathematics. . . . [3]

John Locke was one of the first to advocate the use of similar empirical techniques, observation and measurement, in the discovery of truths about politics, and then Voltaire, who spent a few years in England in the early eighteenth century, carried the news to France. In his *Letters on the English* Voltaire said that Locke, "aided everywhere by the torch of physics," had found a sure method of human knowledge.

The Enlightenment, the age of reason, was pervaded by an optimistic belief in the penetrability of nature's secrets, in the power of the human mind to observe and by observing discover eternal principles. Political philosophy, which had for so long been a kind of by-product of theology, was thought of again as a science. Montesquieu, another French admirer of English scientific method, embarked upon a vast inquiry into politics which included the study of the soils of different nations and which produced an important dictum about political structures—the rule of separation of powers—which was offered and received as a scientific discovery. And because the eighteenth and nineteenth centuries were a time of political revolution as well as of discovery, a period of energetic constitution writing, many of the ideas of Enlightenment philosophers became incorporated into governmental structures. The American Constitution borrowed much from Locke and Montesquieu, as we all know; it is interesting to bear in mind, when we think about science and politics, that our own governmental structure owes a good deal to Newtonian physics.

But all ideas which were once stirring and revolutionary decline with time into dry abstractions, and by the time political science came into its own as an academic discipline in America that belief in the human ability to discover and build had long since lost its fire. Certainly the flame did not burn in academia where, with a few notable exceptions, political science was all legalism and philosophy; to study politics meant either to analyze institutional structures—constitutions, laws, organizational forms—or to browse among the classics and search for nuances of meaning about sovereignty or justice.

This situation existed after World War II, a conflict which at the end, appeared to have been won as much by physicists as by soldiers. At that time a number of political scientists determined to make the discipline more modern and effective and they borrowed, as we have seen, from another academic discipline—psychology—which had already modeled itself upon physics. These behaviorialists decided to create a true political science based on the observation of what human organisms actually *did*. They set out to measure, to work rigorously toward the formulation of empirically verifiable hypotheses and theories. They talked of the need for objectivity and value-free inquiry; they accepted readily the shallow notion that the hard sciences were way ahead of the social sciences, but that with hard work political science might some day catch up. They accepted also the belief that catching up would take awhile. Heinz Eulau has summed up the task before the behavioralists this way:

It is the function of science to understand and interpret the world, not to change it. A science of politics which deserves its name must build from the bottom up by asking simple questions that can, in principle, be answered; it cannot be built from the top down by asking questions that, one has reason to suspect, cannot be answered at all, at least not by the methods of science. An empirical discipline is built by the slow, modest, and piecemeal cumulation of relevant theories and data. The great issues of politics, such as the conditions and consequences of freedom, justice, or authority, are admittedly significant topics, but they are topics compounded with a strong dose of metaphysical discourse. I don't think that they are beyond the reach of behavioral investigation, but before they can be tackled, the groundwork must be laid.[4]

The important thing, it was generally conceded, was to proceed in a scientific, methodical way, and methodology achieved a new importance in the discipline. The stress on the collection of facts generated an unprecedented degree of quantification; political scholars and students found it necessary to become familiar with statistics—and more recently with electrical data processing. Granting that a science required more than the mere accumulation of data, the behavioralists looked for theories that might tie together facts and hypotheses in meaningful ways. They did not attempt to construct vast overarching theories comparable to, for example, the theory of relativity, but settled for "middle-range" theories, mostly adapted from other disciplines; systems theory, communications theory, game theory, decision theory, etc. Although these theories seldom actually explained anything, they had the virtues of a businesslike appearance, a certain unpretentiousness—none of them offered any fundamental challenge to existing perceptions of reality—and a good deal of abstraction.

This new scientific model of political study placed a high value on objectivity and detachment, and redefined the scholar's role so as to split apart the duties of a dispassionate researcher from the sense of self as an involved citizen or as a subjectively experiencing human being. A philosopher, speaking for the logical positivist point of view, wrote: "So long as the philosopher is concerned about his purely theoretical questions, he must forget that he has a human interest as well as a cognitive interest in the object of his investigation."[5] Eulau, whom I have quoted above, has said simply: "Let us not confuse our role of responsible citizen with our role of scientist."[6] The new role definition, as it came to be generally understood, did not preclude political activity by political scientists, but it did demand a separation between research and personal commitment. It presumed that a professor could teach the facts in the classroom and express matters of opinion somewhere else.

In short order the principles of the "behavioral revolution" became the new orthodoxy in American political science.[7] There was opposition, of course. At first the greatest resistance came from conservative scholars who resented the readiness of the new political scientists to throw out the window nearly all of what had gone before—either to disregard it entirely or to make an oversharp distinction between "normative" political philosophy and "empirical" research, between the wispy speculations of the ancients and the hard-nosed realism of the moderns.

The second—the radical—wave of resistance began in the 1960s; it came from a younger generation of students and teachers who talked of relevance and action and commitment, who were inclined to view value-free inquiry as a cop-out from intellectual responsibility, a justification for the bored and useless study of any subject that might produce a grade or a grant. In this new polarization of the discipline the behavioralists—now deeply involved with governmental research and university administration that controlled the powers of the profession itself—were thrown into the conservative role. They were forced to defend the values of science against critics who claimed that in its pursuit of methodological elegance the discipline had turned inward upon itself, lost touch with the needs of students and the society. One such critic warned in 1970 that political scientists were becoming a closed community:

. . . isolated from those they study, researching only those aspects of politics that receive methodological certification. . . . political scientists may come to identify not with the larger political community but with their own ever growing and yet exclusive community. As attention and concern focus inward into the community instead of outward toward the larger political society, we may find ourselves moving once again toward the kind of ivory tower from which behavioralism sought initially to escape. It is a mistake to believe that an ivory tower is a place rather than a frame of mind or a perspective, that it accompanies us in the library but not in the field or research center.[8]

The radical critique alleges that when objective political scientists *do* relate to the political community, they tend to become establishment political scientists—certainly not dissenters against the prevailing power structure, and very likely its paid defenders and servants.

More recently a third line of criticism of the behavioral approach has emerged, and has so many guises that I will refer to it variously as the biological, humanistic, or evolutionary viewpoint. This line of criticism has one thing in common with the spirit of behavioralism, the belief that a scientific search for understanding about society and politics is a perfectly commendable endeavor; its point of dissension is that most social scientists have a very shaky idea of what science really *is*. This evolutionary viewpoint has common areas with the traditionalists also, because it values the use of history and the study of the classics of political philosophy in a historical context. And it has a great deal in common with the radical critique of behavioralism. Its main difference is one of perspective: where the radicals, as we have seen, ask scholars to remember that they are members of the political society, the humanists ask them to remember that they are also members of the human race. In Maslow's terms this viewpoint was expressed as the valuing of people who were "a little less members of their culture, a little more members of their species." In more explicitly ecological terms it reminds scientists that they are themselves living parts of a single biosphere.

One of the few political scientists who has, to my knowledge, addressed himself seriously to the biological dimensions of the discipline is Thomas Landon Thorson. In this chapter I discuss several points raised in his recent book *Biopolitics*.[9]

Thorson's basic thesis is that the social scientists have bought a rather limited and old-fashioned concept of science: the idea that the scientific researcher must observe phenomena and then, by abstracting patterns of behavior, work toward the construction of general laws which, ideally, will allow the prediction of future action. This business of abstracting involves costs—some of the complex reality of nature is always lost in the process of translating it into whatever units and symbols are to be used in theory construction. Such costs are an inherent part of theorizing, abstracting. For Newton the costs were not too great; his physical laws, while less than exact, had a high order of prediction-generalization validity and led toward great technological innovation. The question is, How great are the costs when one tries to apply the prediction-generalization model to human behavior?

Thorson says they are very great indeed. The model is too limiting and tends inevitably to produce conclusions that view human behavior as governed by static, universal laws. One of the models of political analysis which Thorson discusses in this respect is David Easton's "systems" approach, probably the most popular of the "middle-range" theories of behavioralism.[10] The systems approach seeks to work with political phenomena as sets of interrelated variables, and toward this end it views the political system as a kind of vast machine. "We might," says Easton, "compare a political system to a huge and complex factory . . . " Alternatively, Easton describes the system as "a gigantic communications network into which information in the form of demands is flowing and out of which a different kind of information we call a decision emerges."[11]

Now obviously this kind of a perspective upon the political process lends itself admirably to the agenda for behavioral work outlined by Eulau: the system is vast, and there are many areas which can be studied and be expected to yield useful data and specialized hypotheses; it contains many interconnected subsystems, so there is much room for the exploration of "linkages" and the possible formulation of larger hypotheses or even general theories. The trouble with all of this kind of thinking, says Thorson, is that it places a great pressure upon would-be theorists to view the system as a static one:

When one opts for the generalization model of science he seeks uniformities, he seeks that which does not change, he seeks sameness. Thus, the bent, the impetus of his theorizing is settled from the outset. Change as change is theoretically irrelevant. The uniformities, the "persistencies" are the standard. Changes are but deviation from the "perfection" described by the theory. Change as change cannot be *explained*, it can only be "accounted for" in terms of the uniformities.[12]

The effort to understand the system *as a system*, then, and to produce generalizations about it acceptable to the academic community as it is now constituted, requires researchers to look at its stable features; it discourages them from regarding it as being continually in a process of change—in short, evolving. It also (and this, as we will see, is most important) discourages them from considering as relevant data the fact that they are *themselves* part of the system, and that whatever they discover will be fed back into it and very possibly change it. The dimension of time, Thorson argues, is not taken seriously:

It is not scientific, but scientifically naive, to attempt to understand politics on the model of nineteenth-century physics. This is true not only because the fit between the model and the phenomena in question is not very close. It is true also because the static model systematically excludes the most important scientifically demonstrated fact about man. For man is, above all, a biological organism and he is what he is because of and through the process of biological and cultural evolution.[13]

What does it mean to take time seriously in thinking about politics? What is the process of "biological and cultural evolution" which determines the nature of the human race? Before we try to deal with these questions, let us pause to tear down a few intellectual fences.

Consider the word *biology*. We have a common understanding of what the word means, we all know more or less what is taught in biology departments, and in normal usage we take the word to define certain *limited* aspects of human behavior. When we talk of biological causes we ordinarily mean unconscious, instinctive causes. But this limited use of the term tends to blind us to the quite self-evident fact that the evolutionary process has also produced human consciousness and human civilization. The traditional meaning of biology deals with a certain process of information transmission, namely the genetic system by which adaptive information is passed from one generation to the next. The wider meaning of biology, which we must now understand, deals with the fact that in the human species much of the information that determines our adaptive behavior is *not* transmitted through the genes but through the medium of the culture—through symbolic communication. As biologist C. H. Waddington summarizes it: "The human system of social communication functions as such an efficient means of transmitting information from one generation to the next that it has become the mechanism on which human evolution mainly depends"[14] Thus if we are to see what the evolutionary perspective involves, we must get out of the habit of asking for a transfer when we have exhausted the *physical, genetic, instinctual* connotations of biology, and stay with it into domains that we have thought of as belonging to sociology, anthropology, history, and political science.

Let me make clear at this point what the evolutionary perspective is *not*: it is not, for one thing, a revival of the once-popular "social Darwinist" philosophy which tried to make evolution a justification for imperialism and laissez-faire economics. Nor is it a case for a new model in which, abandoning physics, we pick up the whole theory of biological evolution and lay it down upon the history of political development. It is not a new *theory* at all, but rather a *perspective*, a kind of intellectual life style; it is a matter of bringing into greater awareness, taking more seriously and integrating into all activities certain things about humanity and the universe which we already assume to be true but normally compartmentalize. It urges us to see political development *itself* as an advanced form of biological evolution, to look at humanity not as a cog in a vast social machine but rather as (in Julian Huxley's phrase) evolution become conscious of itself. It urges us to formulate a new perspective upon the ancient definition by Aristotle (biologist and political philosopher) of humanity as a "political animal." This modern perspective, according to Thorson, shows humanity "as the political animal in a new sense, as the creator of political order."[15]

Political Development

One of the major concerns of contemporary political science which Thorson has discussed in terms of the evolutionary perspective is the field of political development. This is certainly one of the more prestigious areas of specialization in the discipline today; it is fairly new, it is "relevant," and it is taken seriously enough by political policy-makers to give it a high value in the governmental/academic market-place.

Thorson argues that development theory—which is precisely the field we would expect to be sensitive to the time dimension—is seriously locked into a static type of theory building:

> The power of the universal-generalization model . . . is in fact so great that it has had its effect even on recent attempts to describe the stages of political development. When in an ordinary context the question of political development is raised and the demand is made for a theory of political development, the quest immediately begins for a set of *universal stages* of political development. It seems to be taken for granted that the only sort of set of stages that would be acceptable would be a set that accurately described the actual chronological development of *all* societies. What this really amounts to is the bending, so to speak, of the universal-generalization model so that it includes a historical dimension.[16]

Evolutionary theory deals with this problem by differentiating between specific and general evolution, that is, by noting that not all species are evolving along identical lines. This allows for a refinement of what is meant by a "higher" stage of evolution:

Mammals, for example, are more highly evolved than insects, but—and this is the important point—mammals are not descended from insects even though they presumably have somewhere in the abyss of time a common ancestor.[17]

Thus, to apply this to a specific case, there is no scientific reason to assume that southeast Asia should or can evolve toward a Western-style capitalist (or for that matter, Russian or Chinese-style Communist) political order or to assume that its stages of development are at all comparable to those of other nations.

This description may appear to be what I said the evolutionary perspective is not, a simple application of biological theory to a political problem. While the distinction between specific and general evolution is indeed applied to a political development, it is to be understood that we are here working with a higher level of evolution, in which there is present *consciousness of an evolutionary process*. Thus:

Given the power of modern means of communication, no presently underdeveloped area of the world can ever develop "modernity" in quite the way that the West did just because the people of the area cannot but *know*, in some measure at least, how the West developed over the last several hundred years. Looked at as a matter of evolutionary thresholds this situation makes perfect sense. Searching, however, for general laws in this context can end only in vagueness or frustration.[18]

The principle here is fairly simply: knowledge of the process of change becomes data which is fed into decision-making relative to change, thus altering the course of development. It even appears to be, when stated in such terms, quite compatible with systems theory, merely an elaboration, an addition of a feedback loop. Indeed it is, but the elaboration is one of momentous importance, a fundamental shift in perspective. We now see that the mechanism is conscious of itself; evolution, to evoke Huxley's term again, is conscious of itself. And there appears to be a profound connection between consciousness and time; in social development as in individual growth (remember the gestaltist "paradoxical theory of change")[19] awareness leads inevitably to change because awareness already *is* a change.

Thorson discusses this issue primarily in terms of its importance to scientific theory; I would like to examine it here briefly in terms of ideology and contemporary power politics.

The predominant issue of world politics—which has brought us again and again to the brink of atomic war—has been the question of how and in what direction the less-industrialized nations of the world are to develop. Mainly this has been a bipolar struggle; the so-called emerging nations have been given to understand that their progress must proceed along either the Communist or the alternative—call it democratic or capitalistic—model. Part of the vast appeal of communism in this century has been its *evolutionary* nature: Marxist theory is a historical theory, offering what would appear to be a simple and inexorable route of transformation. Capitalism has been forced to develop its own model of change, and political science has helped this cause; we have our own theory of how emerging nations are to emerge—this theory has been severly bruised by the Vietnam experience, but it still holds onto its most central principle, that industrialization is progress.

The leaders on both sides of this struggle have, like true ideological fanatics, exerted enormous pressure upon less powerful peoples in order to make reality fit the theory. The ancient story of Procrustes, who was willing to cut off the legs of people to make them fit his bed, is if anything too mild a simile to employ in this case. And I must concede that the ideologies of both great powers have had their true believers among the small ones—elites impressed by the appeal of doctrine or the prestige and power of nationhood or the materialistic appeal of money and machinery—who have tried to guide their own nations to become more like Russia or the United States. We know this has been true; whether it has changed or will change is something that the future (perhaps future political science) will reveal. As I was writing this chapter I came across the following article in a San Francisco newspaper:

A "Cleaner" Science for Third World Development

By David Perlman, Science Correspondent

Philadelphia

Young scientists from two dozen "Third World" nations of Africa, Asia and Latin America launched a movement here yesterday to chart a new scientific course for their developing countries.

It marked the beginning of an effort to create a revolution far more significant than the political upheavals that have brought at least nominal independence to their territories in recent decades.

The scientists—nearly 150 of them—have set high goals: industrial development without disrupting their cultures; intensive agriculture without crop failures; pest controls without dangerous reliance on DDT; fertility control without forced contraception.

As they expressed it, they are working to escape the "developed" world's paradoxical legacy of progress—a legacy they see as compounded of pollution, overcrowding, alienation, crime and war.[20]

This hint is, to me, an encouraging one—that the world's great powers are losing some of their appeal as models for progress.

Politics and Ecology

Environmental or ecological issues are quite naturally prominent in the evolutionary perspective. Such issues, until recently, have been more or less invisible; until certain problems began to surface as political issues most political scientists simply were not aware of them at all. The water in Lake Erie was not, thanks to the tunnel vision of academia, a problem for political science.

However, as soon as we begin to look at politics from the evolutionary perspective, it follows naturally that we will begin to ask how well a given society is adapting to its environment. It would be most unlikely that we would consider environmental matters to be politically irrelevant, nor could we possibly dismiss such concerns as a mere fad: they are central to what politics is all about, at all times.

When environmental awareness first began to dawn upon political scientists we tried to make it "fit in." I was at one time very concerned to persuade other political scientists that ecological politics could and should be made a "part" of the discipline. After a few more years of thinking about it I am now convinced that, rather than to think of political science as a field that contains some ecological issues, it makes a good deal more sense to think of ecology as a field that contains some political issues.

This is not something that has suddenly become true; political organization has always been a way of adapting to a natural environment, and civilization has always been, in Thorson's term, the "cultural DNA" for the transmission of adaptive information. But it has suddenly become much more evident, has thrust itself so rudely and persistently into human consciousness that it is no longer possible for us to continue to overlook the ecological meaning of political decisions. As we begin to understand fully the implications of the fact that evolution is a matter of communication—of human creation—as well as of genetic transmission, we inevitably realize that the future course of human evolution can and will be shaped by conscious human decisions. And these decisions are and will be political. Now that we can alter natural water systems, manage the interactions among plants and animals, change the chemical composition of the air we breathe, manipulate the human birth and death rates, and *know* we can do these things, we have arrived at a great transition in human history.

Some time ago evolution became conscious of itself; now evolution must become responsible for itself. It is not overstating the case at all, but only making a rather simple observation from an evolutionary perspective, to say that a species which has arrived at this point is fundamentally different from one which has not, and that a world which contains such a species is fundamentally different from one which has not. However fascinating it may be to speculate about the future transformation of humanity, I personally find it more fascinating to look hard at the transformation that has already taken place.

We are still some way from full awareness of what has happened; the facts are before us, but we have not yet assimilated them into our ways of thinking. In a few more years, when biological technology reaches the point—which it is now close to—of being able to control consistently the genetic makeup of unborn human beings (thereby raising a whole host of new political issues), the essential situation will be more obvious, but not basically different. We are already making political decisions which are altering the course of human evolution and the nature of our world environment. The task before all nations will be one of stating and comprehending the alternatives, and making decisions.

As I confront the reality of this situation, I am certainly not swept away by optimism. We are going to have to develop both an enhanced awareness of ourselves as integral parts of the world ecology and at the same time a tremendous intellectual, scientific sophistication about ecological processes and the consequences of technology. We are going to have to formulate alternatives, submit them to democratic decision-making processes, and in many cases make long-term and worldwide plans and policies. This is a formidable task to lay before a political order that, according to some of its critics, is not capable of making any plans at all.[21]

This task is fundamentally a challenge to the human adaptive capability, an evolutionary threshold. It is productive—indeed, necessary—to look at it from an evolutionary perspective, but we must of course remember that there is nothing in what we know of evolution which contains any guarantees about the survival of a given species. We may not meet the challenge in spite of our great technological and intellectual attainments; our museums are full of the relics of species which somehow did not make the grade.

Science in Evolution

Western society has developed some rather clear and demanding ideas about the role of the scientist, and although—like highly socialized members of any culture—we are inclined to take these role expectations as manifestations of some permanent and necessary truth, they are after all human creations, social patterns which have been different in different times, have changed and can change again. The role of the scientist as we define it today involves a dispassionate character, a rigorous and precise intellect, an equally rigorous and precise method of study, and most basically a division between subject and object. To be scientific is to stand outside a thing and study it. With this definition in mind, let us hear Thorson on the evolutionary perspective, science, and politics:

Taking time and evolution seriously can open the door to a genuine science of society, one which is capable of grasping the whole phenomenon of man. This is science not because of what it can be made to look like by the clever mimic, but because it is fundamentally compatible with—indeed a natural and logical extension of—biology, chemistry, and physics. The genetic system of information transmission is ultimately a matter of physics and chemistry. The cultural system of information transmission is different in many ways, but in the final analysis it is tied through evolution to the same natural processes. Whatever deserves the name political science must start with a conception of the human animal in nature and must conclude with an account which will deal with the whole phenomenon of politics, the choosing and creating as well as the reacting and responding.

The classical world, the world of Plato and Aristotle, saw man in nature but it could not see man in time. The Christian world of Augustine and Thomas

Aquinas saw a dichotomy between man's spiritual life and his temporal life, between soul and body, and it saw man in time. A foreshortened but nonetheless linear conception of time is clearly present in Christain thinking—creation, fall, immaculate conception, crucifixion, resurrection, second coming—and the separation of body and soul presages the notion of man's detachment from nature. The modern world—in the historian's sense of modern, say from 1500 A.D.to 1800 A.D.—kept the truncated Christian conception of time but saw man as detached from nature, as artificer *par excellence.*

. . . .

Only in the last hundred years or so could any man have possibly known (1) that man is the product of an evolutionary process stretching back some six billion years, and (2) that man was capable of establishing the detached observer position, of devising modern science and technology, and of creating modern society. Plato, Aristotle, Augustine and Thomas-Aquinas—masters though they were—could not possibly have known of these parameters. Descartes, Hobbes and Locke could see the position of detachment and some of its implications, but by the same token man's connection with the rest of nature had to be rejected and the significance of time could not have been grasped. They were, moreover, too busy creating modern science and modern society to step back and reflect on the implications of the possibility.

Twentieth-century man, however, can see the vastness of time and its overriding significance, man's connection with the natural world through evolution, and the fact of modern culture, its intellectual style and its material product. The recognition of these factors—all of them together—provides a standard, a perspective, utterly unique in human history in terms of which man can decide what he *ought* to do. In this sense a new standard for philosophy and for political philosophy in particular becomes possible. What arises from this perspective is a new understanding of recommendation and justification, a new logic of recommendation, which can only make full sense in the twentieth century.[22]

This redefining of science demands a redefinition of the role of the scientist as well. Part of this redefinition involves discarding the distinction between the social sciences and the physical sciences; it will no longer be necessary for social scientists to play at being "real" scientists, because they will be in fact dealing with the subject matter—especially the long-range consequences—of scientific research. On the other hand it will not be as easy for investigators in the other fields of science to continue to define away their awareness of themselves as living creatures and of their research as part of the greater realm of evolutionary decision-making.

This means not only a change in the socially defined role of the scientist but a change in the consciousness of scientists themselves, a paradigm change of a most profound kind. Scientists will no longer think of themselves as detached from nature, as disembodied intellects in the sense Hannah Arendt meant when she described the rise of modern science as the discovery of the Archimedean point, the place to stand *outside* the world.[23] Rather, they will understand and feel that they are a part—the conscious, deciding, and *responsible* part—of the very evolutionary process they study. It is a fundamental element in the humanistic perspective that objectivity is not necessarily synonymous with the discovery of truth, that real and valuable knowledge can be discovered by human beings who tolerate and in fact seek a fuller awareness of who they are, what they are doing, and how their actions feel emotionally and physically.

This statement may be meaningful to some readers, rather remote and philosophical to others. Let me try to bring it closer to home by talking about the social sciences as they stand right now, and about the issue of relevance.

Amid the growing disillusionment with the academic social sciences, the increasing awareness that a sensitivity to human needs had been lost in the quest for scientific respectability, many social scientists—mainly but by no means exclusively the younger ones—developed a new concern for relevance, a desire to know that their work had some real meaning and value for living people. But because the denial of the value of one's own subjective experience is so central to what our society takes to be the only way of achieving knowledge, because this principle is instilled so deeply in us all, it is sometimes difficult to get a sense of what one ought to be relevant *to*. And consequently those who have wanted to do relevant work have often been vulnerable to radical rhetoric or to mere fashion. This vulnerability is not true for members of racial minority groups, and it is rapidly becoming less true of women—people who see clearly that their own experience provides the impetus and direction for what they are to do as social scientists. But the vast majority of social scientists have failed to make any such connection, and this failure is in a way remarkable evidence of the power of the prohibition against paying attention to one's own felt needs. That the universities of America are full of social scientists breathing the poisoned air of cities, alienated from open personal contact with others, sexually repressed, manipulated by a consumer economy, frustrated by bureaucracy—that there can be people, and there are thousands of them, who live daily with such personal experience and simultaneously wonder what is relevant, is surely one of the great wonders of the modern world. But if we value our personal experience, take it as a source of knowledge, then simultaneously we experience a shift of perspective; we see that the subjects of our inquiry—the world, evolution, culture, the political order—are not simply things "out there" to be abstracted and quantified, but are also ongoing processes "in here" to be felt and comprehended and lived. As we abandon the old schism between the scientific self and the personal self we are confronted with a great new challenge, which is to *integrate* our fragmented and compartmentalized awarenesses into a whole sense of ourselves as feeling, thinking, and acting human beings.

The New Science

So far I have been talking mostly about scientists as individuals, but we need to think about the parameters of science itself, the intellectual form that our new enterprise might take. Thorson, who is far more loyal to his discipline than I am, has uttered a frankly "presumptuous and imperialistic" call for political science "to emerge again as the master science . . . become the interdisciplinary science *par excellence.*" His reasoning follows my own conviction that evolution is becoming increasingly a matter of politics:

> If it is indeed the case that the question of survival will be decided in the next hundred years there is no excuse not to be presumptuous. If man's long, violent history points to the overwhelming necessity of brain power, of the creative use of intelligence; then man's most important animal task, that task which is fundamental to biological survival, is what Aristotle said long ago: reasoning about political and social organization, that enterprise which we have come to call political science.[24]

A somewhat different, though certainly not incompatible, program for a new "science of subjective experience" has been outlined by an interdisciplinary humanist, Willis Harman of Stanford.[25]

> The science of man's subjective experience is in its infancy. Even so, some of its foreshadowings are evident. With the classification of these questions into the realm of empirical inquriy, we can anticipate an acceleration of research in this area. As a consequence there is a new hope of consensus on issues which have been at the root of conflict for centuries (just as earlier there came about consensus on the place of the Earth in the universe, and on the origin of man). The new science will incorporate the most penetrating insights of psychology, the humanities, and religion. These developments will have profound impacts on goal priorities in society, on our concepts of education, on the future development and use of technology, and perhaps (as in the case of the Copernican revolution) on the distribution of power among social institutions and interest groups.[26]

Harman's ideas about the new science include many of the concerns which we have already dealt with in our discussion of various schools of humanistic psychology. He mentions the following as some of the probable characteristics:

> Although we have been speaking of it as a science of subjective experience, one of its dominant characteristics will be a relaxing of the subjective-objective dichotomy. . . .
> Related to this will be the incorporation, in some form, of the age-old yet radical doctrine that we perceive the world and ourselves in it as we have been culturally "hypnotized" to perceive it. The typical commonsense-scientific view of reality will be considered to be a valid but partial view. . . .
> The new science . . . will include some sort of mapping or ordering of states of consciousness transcending the usual conscious awareness. . . .
> It will include a much more unified view of the processes of personal change and emergence which take place within the contexts of psychotherapy, education (in the sense of "know thyself"), and religion (as spiritual growth). This view will possibly center around the concept that personality and behavior patterns change consequent upon a change in self-image, a modification of the person's emotionally felt perception of himself and his relationship to his environment.[27]

As we view the outlines of such a new science it is natural to ask, What about behavioralism? What about all the work that has been done in the social sciences as they have been defined, now, for nearly twenty years? Personally I do not think the products of the behavioral epoch are to be thrown out the window, any more than I could ever agree with those behavioralists who thought their new approach had suddenly rendered useless all of prior political philosophy. If I have learned anything at all from the growth principles of humanistic psychology, it is that you work from where you are and not from where you think you ought to be. And part of the task before us is to integrate what we have learned from behavioral research into a wider—and more complex—perspective. The vastness of this project was suggested recently by Ludwig von Bertalanffy—whom I have cited earlier[28] as the father of the same general systems theory which somehow found its way into political science as the model of the "social factory"—when he said:

The problems of biological research are much richer than the stereotype of "laws of physics and chemistry" plus "selection." They surely will require not less but probably much more scientific ingenuity and sophistication than theoretical physics. In its philosophical aspects, this amounts . . . to the replacement, or rather the generalization of the Newtonian universe of blind forces and isolable causal trains, and of Darwinian living nature as a product of chance, by an organismic universe of many levels, the laws of which are a challenge to future research.[29]

Notes

[1]George Steiner, "Life-Lines," New Yorker, 6 March 1971, p. 101.

[2]For an account of the "scientism" controversy, see Albert Somit and Joseph Tannenhaus, The Development of American Political Science (Boston: Allyn and Bacon, 1967).

[3]Carl Becker, The Declaration of Independence (New York: Harcourt, Brace Jovanovich, Inc. 1922), pp. 41–42.

[4]Heinz Eulau, The Behavioral Persuasion in Politics (New York: Random House, Inc. and Pantheon Books, a Division of Random House, Inc. 1963), p. 10.

[5]Morris Schlick, "What Is the Aim of Ethics?" in Logical Positivism ed. A. J. Ayer (Glencoe, Ill.: Free Press, 1960), p. 247.

[6]In James C. Charlesworth, ed., A Design for Political Science: Scope, Objectives and Methods, (Philadelphia: American Academy of Political and Social Science, 1956), p. 115.

[7]Although I have borrowed the term behavioral revolution, which is commonly used in discussion about what happened to political science, I do not believe it was a revolution at all but rather a belated and localized conversion to the prevailing cultural values of the time. True revolutions are a good deal riskier.

[8]J. Peter Euben, "Political Science and Political Silence," in Power and Community: Dissenting Essays in Political Science eds. Phillip Green and Sanford Levinson (New York: Pantheon Books, a Division of Random House, Inc. 1970) pp. 43–44.

[9]From Biopolitics by Thomas Landon Thorson. Copyright © 1970 by Holt, Rinehart and Winston, Inc. Reprinted by permission of Holt, Rinehart and Winston, Inc.

[10]Ironically, general systems theory was originally a biological theory, an outgrowth of the work of Ludwig von Bertalanffy. The theory as adapted into political science was primarily abstract and mechanistic, which it would not have been if Easton had investigated further the thinking of von Bertalanffy—who is both a biologist and a humanistic psychologist. See, for example, von Bertalanffy, "The World of Science and the World of Value," in Challenges of Humanistic Psychology ed. J. F. T. Bugental (New York: McGraw-Hill, 1967), pp. 335–344.

[11]David Easton, *A Systems Analysis of Political Life* (New York: John Wiley and Sons, 1965), p. 72.

[12]*Biopolitics*, p. 52.

[13]*Ibid.*, pp. 81–82.

[14]C. H. Waddington, *The Ethical Animal* (London: George Allen & Unwin Ltd. 1961), p. 7.

[15]*Biopolitics*, p. 119.

[16]*Ibid.*, pp. 141–142. Italics in original.

[17]*Ibid.*, p. 141.

[18]*Ibid.*, p. 148.

[19]See above, p. 48.

[20]*San Francisco Chronicle*, 28 December 1971.

[21]See Theodore J. Lowi, *The End of Liberalism* (New York: W. W. Norton, 1969).

[22]*Biopolitics*, pp. 178–180.

[23]Hannah Arendt, *The Human Condition* (Chicago: University of Chicago Press, 1958).

[24]Thorson, "The Biological Foundations of Political Science: Reflections on the Post-Behavioral Era," paper, 1970 annual meeting, American Political Science Association.

[25]Dr. Harman is director of the Center for the Study of Social Policy at Stanford Research Institute and professor of engineering and economic systems, Stanford University.

[26]Willis W. Harman, "The New Copernican Revolution," *Stanford Today*, Winter, 1969, Series II, No. 1.

[27]*Ibid.*, pp. 130–131.

[28]See footnote 10.

[29]Von Bertalanffy, "Chance or Law," in *Beyond Reductionism: New Perspectives in the Life Sciences* eds. Arthur Koestler and J. R. Smythies (Boston: Beacon Press, 1971), p. 76.

IX. Consciousness and Political Action

Sociology has yielded to psychology as the generative principle of revolution. Consciousness, not class, is now taken to be the root of social reality. . . .

—Theodore Roszak[1]

Thomas Kuhn's book on *The Structure of Scientific Revolutions* has become a kind of underground—perhaps even above-ground—classic; many people find it important and exciting because of what it says about the human processes that go along with scientific discovery. It speaks, with considerable historical authority, of how new paradigms—fundamentally different ways of seeing and ordering experience—periodically emerge to transform not only a body of science but often the consciousness of all humanity. Kuhn describes scientific breakthroughs in words that curiously resemble descriptions of the satori of Zen or the "aha!" experience of psychotherapy:

Scientists . . . often speak of the "scales falling from the eyes" or of the "lightning flash" that "inundates" a previously obscure puzzle, enabling its components to be seen in a new way that for the first time permits its solution. . . . No ordinary sense of the term "interpretation" fits these flashes of intuition through which a new paradigm is born.[2]

This kind of experience is rather different from the impersonal image of scientists which pervades American culture, and certainly different from the image which has been accepted in the social sicences. Consider the words of Clark Hull, eminent behavior psychologist, who cautioned against the contamination of scientific work by what he called "anthropomorphic subjectivism" and insisted that, "A genuinely scientific theory no more needs the anthropomorphic intuition of the theorist to eke out the deduction of its implications than an automatic calculating machine needs the intuitions of the operator in the determination of a quotient, once the keys representing the dividend and the divisor have been depressed."[3]

Kuhn's view differs from the mechanistic image of science not merely because he points up the important role played by human intuition; he also gives us a rather different picture of the situation that exists before a scientific breakthrough occurs. In the image of science offered by such writers as Hull, the period prior to scientific discovery is characterized by the absence of data; as new data become available, new knowledge and understanding naturally follow. But Kuhn shows several instances where scientists had all the data available for a new discovery but literally could not *see* it until the inconsistencies in the existing paradigm forced a total reintegration of thought and experience, a new *gestalt* which, in explaining the data, also gave it the right to exist. Then, when a new explanatory system comes into existence it not only deals with existing information in a new way; it also opens new areas for research because things which had previously been invisible now become visible and make sense: "During revolutions scientists see new and different things when looking with familiar instruments in places they have looked before."[4]

Freud considered his psychoanalytic theory a new paradigm, which equaled the discoveries of Galileo and Darwin in its ability to force people to restructure their image of the universe and how the human race stood in relation to it. When we view politics within the Freudian paradigm, we see society as a huge stage for the acting out of internal conflict, a hopeless war between the deep inner needs of individuals and the needs of the system. The behaviorist movement did not offer any such dramatic new paradigm—in part because it was essentially a restatement of what had been a dramatic new paradigm in the seventeenth century: the image of the universe as a smoothly spinning machine, guided by hard and discoverable natural laws. But although the behaviorist movement produced no single new political theory, it has tended to convey a fairly coherent view of political behavior stressing power and economic motivations, to view society as a kind of vast machine, and to deal with individuals in terms of their social roles and group memberships.

Just as Freud believed that his discoveries about the unconscious brought an entire new world-view into existence, so humanistic psychologists believe that their discoveries about the growth and integrative possibilities of men and women are not simply additional psychological data but the basis of an entire redefinition of humanity. Maslow, whose work on self-actualization was a part of this, saw the third force as more of a world-view than a school of psychology; he called it "a Zeitgeist, a spirit of the age, a change of basic thinking along the total front of man's endeavors, a potential change in every social institution. . . ."[5]

All of the humanistic theories that we have discussed in this book seem to indicate that the process of personal growth, especially as it moves into the higher reaches of human potentiality, includes some kind of a transformation of the individual's relation to the social order, cultural norms, laws, ideology, and institutions. This transformation has been suggested by some, fairly explicitly stated by others. But no third-force psychologist has attempted to work out a systematic theory of consciousness and politics, to make clear how the kind of personal development that the movement is studying and helping to bring about may affect American society—or how American society may affect it. It was inevitable, though, if the third force was at all the Zeitgeist Maslow believed it to be, that such work would begin to appear, as indeed it has: Charles Reich's book *The Greening of America* is one effort in this direction and another—which I discuss at some length in this chapter—is Charles Hampden-Turner's *Radical Man*.[6]

By "radical man" Hampden-Turner means both a human being who is capable of radical political action and views, and also a radically new and different image of politics and human interaction generally. Fundamental to the idea of radical man is the thesis that the social sciences as they stand conspire to force us to think of humanity in terms that are essentially conservative. The conspiracy is not the deliberate product of ideological conservatism—in fact most of the conspirators are political liberals—but rather the unexpected yet inevitable result of the use of "scientific" methodology. Hampden-Turner calls it "the borrowed toolbox" and says, "We should not deceive ourselves that the borrowed toolbox is neutral. Those tools regarded as most 'scientific' uncover selectively those aspects of man that most resemble the dead mechanical universe for which the tools were originally designed."[7]

This produces not merely a certain insensitivity toward the process of change (as we discussed in the last chapter) but a kind of invisible conservatism that follows naturally from the impersonal approach to the study of how people act:

The need to predict and control produces detachment, an unequal relationship and a self-fulfilling prophecy which makes the unequal appear undeserving of equality. . . . The demand for precision and invariability attracts the investigator to the more trivial and repetitive activities of man. . . . Empiricism focuses on stereotyped externalities, ignores depth of experience and emphasizes the status quo above visions of the future. . . . Analysis fragments without being able to reintegrate, looks to the past instead of facing forward, regards man in the light of animals and fails to respect his complexity. The "games" which simulate life view it as a competitive struggle for scarce resources, rather than the synergistic creation of abundance.

Now there is a simple political term which sums up this orientation. It is *conservative*. And those who doubt me can examine McClosky's painstaking research on the conservative personality. . . . An American conservative is elitist, hierarchical, and anxious to control others. He tends to see mankind as animalistic and as an unorganized rabble. He is often vigorous but is obsessive and repetitive in his habits. He values consensus and discipline. He is suspicious of unpredictable people and has little tolerance for human ambiguity, sees life as an economic struggle, looks to the past, and tends to stereotype people. He is uneasy with emotion and affect, prefers to put social distance between himself and others and to withdraw into a class of like-minded people.

It will be immediately objected that social scientists give little support to conservatism and are actively disliked on the American Right. Quite so. Like any academics they need the liberal ideology of free inquiry and the search for truth. . . . Their social conservatism is *for others*, the objects of investigation. Moreover their conservatism is latent in the tools they employ. It comes about less by valuing conservatively than by the "value-free" selection of the less than human. . . . He who is silent assents, and to describe the status quo with detailed and passionless precision is usually to dignify it.[8]

In making this argument Hampden-Turner is in the same camp with a number of people who have noted that academic political science was taken completely off guard by the protest movements of the 1960s and the liberation movements of the 1970s and still has trouble dealing with evidence of idealistic behavior or seriously considering the possibility that any really fundamental change can or will take place in American society.[9]

Where Hampden-Turner begins to move into new territory is in his assertion that the hard-science methodology not only produces limitations, but subtly constructs a certain picture of what it means to be a human being: "What the borrowed toolbox uncovers and helps to create is Conservative Man."[10] And he argues that it is possible to take a fresh and hard look at the evidence that is before us all and discern a different human image; he calls it radical man:

> While Conservative Man is caused to behave, Radical Man imagines and reasons autonomously. Where the former responds predictably and obediently, the latter rebels creatively. Where the former is a product of natural forces, the latter defines himself and his environment in dialogue with others and is a radiating center of meaning. Where the former seeks to *conserve* his energy, reduce dissonance and achieve equilibrium, the latter seeks to create more energy, and values the tension and excitement of disequilibrium.[11]

Hampden-Turner's discovery of Radical Man in politics is precisely parallel to, and in part inspired by, Maslow's discovery of self-actualizing people in psychology. Just as Maslow believed that psychology had become so preoccupied with human sickness that it was blind to human health, so does Hampden-Turner argue that the social sciences in general had so successfully directed their attention to men and women as cogs in the power-driven, wealth-manipulating system that they could not see men and women as capable of any truly creative or idealistic social action. And, just as Maslow did not want to let the discovery of health carry us to the other blindness, an incapacity to deal with the obstacles to growth and the symptoms of mental stress, Hampden-Turner does not ask us to believe that all political action is creative or synergistic.

Maslow, it should be remembered, did not simply divide the human race into the self-actualized and the non-self-actualized. Rather, he tried to show that the drive toward self-actualization was a real and identifiable biological force which operates to some degree in us all:

> Every human being has *both* sets of forces within him. One set clings to safety and defensiveness out of fear, tending to regress backward, hanging on to the past, *afraid* to grow away from the primitive communion with the mother's uterus and breast, *afraid* to take chances, *afraid* to jeopardize what he already has, *afraid* of independence, freedom and separateness. The other set of forces impels him forward toward wholeness of Self and uniqueness of Self, toward full functioning of all his capacities. . . . [12]

Hampden-Turner, similarly, does not offer radical man as a substitute for the prevailing image of humanity, but rather as the other side of the coin. "What we have . . . is a principle of complementarity in which two opposing conceptualizations of man are required to organize the findings of social science."[13] The perspective on the psychology of political action which he outlines—and which he describes as a process of "psycho-social development"—is not simply bipolar: good guys and bad guys. It is an attempt to understand how human beings may grow and flourish and create in the social order—and also how they may stop, hold fast to whatever they think they have got, and fail to deal creatively with the present or the future.

At the risk of oversimplifying from the complexity of the theory and research in *Radical Man*, I am going to select out of it one theme—the interpretation of political orientations in terms of psychosocial development. I discuss this theme here as (1) a logical extrapolation into specifically political terms of some of the ideas of the humanistic psychologists, and (2) as an example of how the humanistic perspective is capable of generating strikingly different explanations of what goes on in politics.

The term *psychosocial development* is a bridge between psychology and politics. It defines Hampden-Turner's basic theoretical proposition which is that, as a person grows and develops, he or she continually re-creates or redefines his or her relationship to other people and to society as a whole. The person develops both a greater inner autonomy and a greater openness to others. One body of research which Hampden-Turner sees as a partial illustration of this process is Lawrence Kohlberg's cognitive-developmental approach to socialization theory, which describes the process of individual learning in terms of "processes of *interaction* between the structure of the organism and the structure of the environment." The growing individual, developing an increasing capacity to feel and understand, creates new and more complex comprehensions of the environment and new ways of functioning in it. The general line of growth is toward a sense of "reciprocity between the self's actions and those of others toward the self." And this developing sense of reciprocity is the "definer of morality, conceived as principles of justice. . . . "[14] Thus, according to Kohlberg, the process of human development involves a growing awareness of principles of relationship to the environment; growth can be conceptualized in *moral* stages, "successive forms of reciprocity, each more differentiated and universalized than the preceding form."[15]

This development was organized in terms of six distinct stages of growth, identified as follows:

Stage 1: Obedience and punishment orientation. Egocentric deference to superior power or prestige. . . .

Stage 2: Naively egoistic orientation. Right action is that instrumentally satisfying the self's needs and occasionally others'. . . .

Stage 3: Good-boy orientation. Orientation to approval and to pleasing and helping others. Conformity to stereotypical images of majority or natural role behavior. . . .

Stage 4: Authority and social-order maintaining orientation. Orientation to "doing duty" and to showing respect for authority and maintaining the given social order for its own sake. . . .

Stage 5:Contractual legalistic orientation. Recognition of an arbitrary element or starting point in rules or expectations for the sake of agreement. Duty defined in terms of contract, general avoidance of violation of the will or rights of others. . . .

Stage 6: Conscience or principle orientation. Orientation not only to actually ordained social rules but to principles of choice involving appeal to logical universality and consistency. . . . [16]

The research out of which this scale emerged was designed to test the different ways people responded to moral problems. Given a specific fictional situation to work with, different individuals would reveal different ways of comprehending the meaning or justification of their response to it. For example, in a typical case, subjects were asked to imagine the situation of a man whose wife needs a certain drug which will save her life. The drug is available only from a supplier who demands a price far beyond the subject's ability to pay. In this situation subjects would typically respond that stealing the drug was justified. But there was enormous difference in *how* they conceptualized the justification. Ordered in terms of the above stages, these varied as follows:

At Stage 1, the individual is primarily motivated by the desire to avoid punishment by a superior power: *God would punish me if I let my wife die. My father-in-law would make trouble for me.*

At Stage 2, concern has shifted to the satisfaction of quasi-physical needs. The individual develops an awareness of the relative value of each person's needs as his own drives are frustrated by demands for exchange and reciprocity: *I have a right to the services of my wife, and naturally this is more important than whatever rights the druggist may claim. No one is going to look out for my interest or my wife's unless I do.*

The conventional orientation of Stages 3 and 4 involves conformity to traditional role expectations and maintenance of existing social and legal order. The Stage-3 individual is motivated to avoid social disapproval for nonconformity and would like to be judged by his intentions: *I'd do what any half-decent husband would do—save his family and carry out his protective function.*

The Stage-4 person understands how his role fits into larger constellations of roles, the institutions approved by others. He seeks to perform his duty—to meet the expectations of society: *My wife and I submitted ourselves to a higher law, the institution of marriage. The fabric of our society is held together by this institution. I know my lawful duty when I see it.*

The two postconventional stages represent the most advanced levels of moral development. Decisions are based on consideration of shared values rather than on self-centered interests or blind conformity to external standards. The Stage-5 individual perceives his duty in terms of a social contract, recognizing the arbitrary nature of rules made for the sake of agreement. He avoids infringing on the rights of others, or violating the welfare of the majority: *My wife and I promised to love and help one another whatever the circumstances. We chose to make the commitment and in our daily lives together it is constantly renewed. I am therefore committed to saving her.*

The Stage-6 person relies heavily on his own conscience and the mutual respect of others. He recognizes the universal principles that underlie social commitments and seeks to apply them as consistent principles of moral judgment: *No contract, law, obligation, private gain or fear of punishment should impede any man from saving those he loves. For the sake of my wife I will steal the drug; for the sake of others who might share my experience, I will steal the drug publicly, so that society may cease to sacrifice human relationships to the profit motive.*[17]

Before we proceed to the more specifically political aspects of this research, let us stop to note how it differs from Freudian and behaviorist models of socialization. In Freudian theory, the foundation and source of morality is the superego, the forcefully internalized norms of the culture which are forever in conflict with the potentially savage instinctual drives. In behaviorist theory, such as Skinner's, there is really only one principle of reciprocity, which is that the environment controls all individuals by dispensing negative and positive reinforcements, and every person tries to figure out how to get the most of whatever feels the best. But in Kohlberg's view—which becomes the basis of Hampden-Turner's theory of political behavior—people strive naturally toward greater synergy with their environment, and in so doing they create concepts of reciprocity which are in fact moral principles.

Hampden-Turner equates Kohlberg's levels of moral judgment whith levels of psychosocial development. Each of the stages, he says, has its corresponding stage of political consciousness. You will find most conservatives at Stages 3 or 4; most liberals at Stage 5, and *some* radicals at Stage 6.[18]

The person functioning at the Stage-3 level of development is one who is operating according to the patterns outlined by sociologists in the theory of roles—that is, he or she is behaving according to certain socially defined models and generally in accordance with the expectations of others. Hampden-Turner finds a predominance of female conservatives at this stage.

At Stage 4 the individual begins to see that his or her role is only a part of a vast system of roles and rules which are defined and protected by legitimate authority. Morality is a matter of upholding and defending this system. Male conservatives.

At Stage 5 the person perceives that the system is a human creation, a matter of an agreed-upon relationship among groups and individuals, a contractual *relationship* to which he or she is a consenting partner, with both benefits and obligations. This stage is characteristically a liberal political orientation.

At Stage 6 the individual operates from a felt and comprehended sense of fundamental moral principles; he or she follows these principles freely and individually, without the necessity of social contract or role expectations. This kind of orientation, representing the highest levels of psychosocial development, is what Hampden-Turner calls "developmental radicalism." In action it is revealed by such characteristics as intense investment in the human environment, a capacity to risk oneself, a desire to bridge the distance to communicate with others, openness to experience, and a continuing drive to integrate feedback from experience into new, changed, and increasingly complex mental matrices.[19] Its political manifestation can be, when the occasion requires, some form of radical behavior: such individuals will if necessary discard roles, violate laws, and even break through the limitations of existing social contracts.

At this point Hampden-Turner's work probably appears to be a pure hymn to radicalism. In order to correct such a possible misinterpretation I should make it clear that the theory and research does not automatically place all radicals at Stage 6. One of the most important characteristics of the true "developmental radical" is an authentic desire and ability to communicate—to reach out to others, enter their minds and enhance their lives. But in research with students involved in the Berkeley Free Speech Movement he found that, while many of the leaders of the FSM appeared to be true Stage 6 radicals, there were others who fell far short of this and in fact showed many of the characteristics of Stage 2. He noted their "coldness, aloofness, stubbornness, and relative unconcern for sensitivity and responsiveness to others," the inability or unwillingness to make rebellion an act of *communication*.[20]

The intent of *Radical Man* is not simply to elevate radical political behavior but to provide a different paradigm, a new way of looking at it. The other models which we have considered tend to stress radicalism as *deviance*: in Freudian analysis it inevitably becomes the irrational acting out of authority problems; behavioral approaches see only the individual's failure to function in the social role and the social system. The humanistic paradigm which Hampden-Turner offers describes system-transcending and self-transcending behavior as healthy—not a deviation, but a natural expression of the capacity for growth inherent in men and women.

This is not to deny the fact that political conservatives do not come off too well in Hampden-Turner's system; conservatism is quite clearly seen as reflecting a less advanced stage of personal development. Indeed, the whole country falls rather short as seen from his viewpoint: "What clearly emerges from research . . . is that the vast majority of American adults and school children have only reached Stages 3 to 4. They are rarely capable of making principled moral judgments and do not even comprehend these judgments when others make them."[21]

There is a value in social roles and social structure, but it is a *developmental* value; the theory we have been discussing here is one of growth, and it holds "that children and young adults in the process of socialization and moral growth learn each stage in sequence." Thus the "conservative truths" at Stages 3 and 4 can be seen as a "kind of heuristic device by which the developing person learns to 'home in' upon the needs of the other. It is like learning to swim with a pair of water-wings. Later these are discarded, for they actually impede the good swimmer, but without them the task of learning might be considerably harder.''[22]

This appears to lend itself to an extremely radical view of political history. Conventionally the decline of a social institution is seen as the ultimate evidence of its failure; but in a developmental view we might see it as just the opposite: a social order which produces people capable of discarding it and creating a new social order might be judged to have succeeded admirably in its purpose. The dissolution of the British Empire over which Winston Churchill was so unwilling to preside might be seen as the most brilliant evidence of the empire's productivity.

In any case Hampden-Turner's view of the role of institutions in psychosocial development is certainly in the same spirit as humanistic psychotherapy. This spirit was expressed best by Carl Rogers, who always insisted that the goal of therapy was autonomy, that the therapist must always strive to become obsolete. Similarly, the role model of the self-actualized person, the rules of gestalt therapy, the creative social-contact atmosphere of the encounter group, all have their developmental value—but the person who remains hung up on the role model, the rules, or the group, has not learned from them. The same spirit can be found in Zen: at first the student is awed by the masters and by the tradition they embody, but in the end the student laughs at them—and they take that irreverence as evidence of their success.

Although it does seem to be true that the progress of individuals may be arrested at any one of the developmental stages, each of the stages should in some way facilitate growth, provide something that the person needs. This harmonizes with Maslow's description of the hierarchy of needs, in which satisfaction at each point contributes to further growth, and also with Kenneth Keniston's research with student dissenters, in which he found young radicals to be not bitter outcasts, but rather the products of lives of abundance and security.[23]

The system also relates to the situation of minorities; in recognizing the developmental value of roles and social structures it recognizes that roles and structures must have *value* and *meaning* for the individuals who are expected to participate in them. The social roles traditionally available to blacks and other racial minorities, or to women, may have excellent system-maintenance value but they contribute relatively little to the psychosocial development of the individuals who occupy them. And if the social roles open to members of such minorities are rather unproductive, so the role-models made available by the culture are rather uninspiring. In spite of some recent hurried tokenism from the mass media, the heroes of American history and culture still average out to be white, middle-class, male, and relentlessly heterosexual. We can understand, then, why leaders of the liberation movements go back into history again to find blacks and Indians and Chicanos and women and homosexuals who in their personal lives transcended the cultural stereotypes; even these role-models may be discarded in time, but they fill a real and felt developmental need.

If we are to use the concept of psychosocial development, then we must realize that roles, systems of law and order, social contracts, cannot be *imposed*. Unless individuals can invest themselves deeply in social roles, see wisdom and fairness in the social order, then such structures will have no value as facilitators of human growth.

There is a need for human creativity—which may involve risks and radical action—to pour meaning into structures. The developmental perspective sees that the individuals who operate at the highest level of growth do not only break free of the social order but also contribute to its renewal:

> In a certain sense the Stage 6 "radicals of conscience" have *transcended the dichotomy between radicalism and conservatism*. Their act of conscience ideally should be capable of becoming a shared contract (Stage 5), a good law (Stage 4), an appropriate role (Stage 3), an occasion for personal satisfaction (Stage 2), and a reward or punishment appropriate to circumstances (Stage 1). Only the individual conscience, comprehending as it does all the lower stages, can keep the "radical" and the "conservative" aspects of the social and personal systems in an active unity, providing each person and group with that which it most lacks.[24]

Another dichotomy transcended is that between, on the one hand, personal autonomy, individualism, inner-directedness, even idiosyncracy and, on the other, unselfishness, concern for others, openness, flexibility, acceptance, awareness. Hampden-Turner's model of psychosocial development (as well as the supporting work of Kohlberg, Piaget, and others) views human growth as a continual restructuring by the organism of its relationship to the environment.

What follows naturally from this is a field or gestalt theory of political science. We cannot simply talk about the "psychological factors" in political behavior or consider any system of human development out of the context of the environments of individuals; nor can we make much sense out of the environment—group membership, class, economic and social factors—unless we are prepared to differentiate among the many ways an environment can be organized in the consciousness of a person.

Ultimately social science must begin to see, as do growing individuals, that the person and the enviornment are quite inseparable, simply different facets of a single process.

Notes

[1]Theodore Roszak: "Counter Culture IV: The Future as Community," (see ch. 5, fn. 10), p. 499.

[2]Thomas Kuhn, *The Structure of Scientific Revolutions* (Chicago: University of Chicago Press, 1970), p. 122.

[3]Clark Hull, *Principles of Behavior: An Introduction to Behavior Theory* (New York: Appleton-Century-Crofts 1943), p. 24.

[4]Kuhn, *Structure of Revolutions*, p. 111.

[5]Maslow, foreword to Frank Goble, *The Third Force* (New York: Grossman, 1970), p. ix.

[6]I emphasize *Radical Man* here because it is explicitly a work of synthesis, ordering vast amounts of existing social science data into the conceptualizations of humanistic

psychology. Another recent book which performs a similar task is Jeanne N. Knutson, *The Human Basis of the Polity* (Chicago: Aldine-Atherton, 1972).

[7]Charles Hampden-Turner, *Radical Man* (Cambridge, Mass. Schenkman Books 1971), p. 17.

[8]*Ibid.*, pp. 17–18. (Italics in original.) The research cited is H. McClosky, "Conservatism and Personality," *American Political Science Review*, 42 (1958).

[9]See John H. Schaar, "Legitimacy in the Modern State," in Green and Levinson, *Dissenting Essays* (see ch. 8, fn. 8), pp. 276–327.

[10]Hampden-Turner, *Radical Man*, p. 17.

[11]*Ibid.*, p. 17.

[12]A. Maslow, *Toward a Psychology of Being*, p. 41.

[13]Hampden-Turner, *Radical Man*, p. 17.

[14]Lawrence Kohlberg, "Stage and Sequence: The Cognitive-Developmental Approach to Socialization," in *Handbook of Socialization Theory and Research* Ed. David A. Goslin © 1969 by Rand McNally & Company, Chicago; p. 347 passim.

[15]*Ibid.*, p. 398. Kohlberg acknowledges a number of theoretical sources to his work, of which perhaps the most important is Piaget. See Jean Piaget, *The Moral Judgment of the Child* (1932).

[16]*Ibid.*, p. 376.

[17]Hampden-Turner, and Phillip Whitten, "Morals Left and Right," Excerpted from *Psychology Today* magazine. Copyright © 1971 Communications/Research/Machines, Inc.

[18]The discussion of this system in this chapter is based mostly on published material as cited, partly on material presented by Hampden-Turner at meetings of the American Political Science Association and the Association for Humanistic Psychology, partly on personal conversations and partly on my own interpretations. As a general rule I suggest that readers who are outraged by the whole thing attack Hampden-Turner for everything quoted or attributed to him specifically, and me for the rest.

[19]*Radical Man*, p. 37.

[20]*Ibid.*, pp. 324–325.

[21]*Ibid.*, p. 138. Hampden-Turner believes that as a general rule people are capable of comprehending only one stage above their own customary level of judgment: to an individual operating at Stage 3 or 4, Stage 6 behavior is quite incomprehensible and can only be interpreted as reflecting a lower—usually Stage 2—level of development.

[22]*Ibid.*, p. 323.

[23]Kenneth Keniston, *Young Radicals: Notes on Committed Youth* (New York: Harcourt, Brace, Jovanovich, 1968).

[24]*Radical Man*, p. 325.

X. On The State As A State Of Mind

A revolution is currently going on in relation to sanity and madness, both inside and outside psychiatry.

—R. D. Laing[1]

The social function of the Inquisition and of Institutional Psychiatry lies in the service each renders its society; both provide an intellectually meaningful, morally uplifting, and socially well-organized system for the ritualized affirmation of the benevolence, glory and power of society's dominant ethic.

—Thomas Szasz[2]

Let us explore the idea that "the establishment" or "the power structure" can be viewed as an established consciousness, a psychological power structure. Let us say that all social institutions rest upon how people think and feel, how they comprehend the *meaning* of being human, how they experience the self, how they perceive their relationship to the environment and to each other. Let us say that the social order is perpetuated by training people to think in its terms—by educating and socializing the young and by maintaining some form of psychological control over all people as they mature. Let us say that the state, in short, is a state of mind.

In discussing this notion—which, by the way, is not particularly new or extreme—I want it understood that the consciousness which must be instilled and maintained in order to perpetuate a given social order is not merely the individual's understanding of things political; rather, let us say that the social order rests upon far deeper and broader foundations, upon the most basic and fundamental ways that people conceive of what is real and rational. And let us remember that, although such basic conceptions of realness and rationality always seem irrefutably and obviously *so* from inside, they vary enormously from culture to culture and from era to era. They can change.

The perspective which I am describing here could as easily be called cultural as psychological: it is expressed in various ways by anthropologists, by those political scientists who emphasize the cultural bases of institutions, and by such contemporary analysts as Theodore Roszak, who has described the emergence of a counterculture—which is essentially a shared consciousness—among the American young.[3] However, I want to look at the matter from a psychological perspective here, because some particularly interesting things are going on in the fields of clinical psychology and psychiatry.

In spite of all the efforts of psychiatrists to maintain that their profession is an objective, ideologically neutral science, political issues seem to be turning up in it with increasing frequency. Dr. Seymour Halleck has described the debate which is going on within the American psychiatric profession. On one side are the conservatives, such as the 1971–1972 president of the American Psychiatric Association, Dr. Ewald Busse, who says:

> It is my opinion that psychiatric services should not be the tool for restructuring society or solving economic problems or for determining new human values. Psychiatric services should be continued as patient oriented activities designed to reduce pain and discomfort and to increase the capacity of the individual to adjust satisfactorily. . . . [4]

On the other side are the liberals, such as Dr. Raymond Waggoner, a past president of the same association, who says:

> I plead for a psychiatry that is involved with fundamental social goals. I plead for a psychiatry that will eschew isolation altogether and assume its proper leadership role in advancing the total health of our nation. I plead for a psychiatry that is at once concerned with individual liberty and communal responsibility and I ask of psychiatrists that they be not only pragmatists but also dreamers with a vision of the future.[5]

This is a fairly mild argument, as we will see when we get to some further thoughts on this subject, and yet it represents what I consider to be the basic cleavage. The two speakers have crept cautiously to opposing positions on the issue of whether psychotherapy should help the individual change to meet society's expectations or whether society itself, if it causes people to suffer psychological stress, must be changed. The gap is small, but it is there: it is the gap between working to maintain the system and working to clear the way for human growth, wherever that may lead.

The issue becomes clearer as we look at more extreme statements. The following is from an article by a behavior-modification psychologist advocating massive use of psychological techniques to deal with crime. He is still talking about therapy as adjustment, but here the social-control aspect of it becomes more explicit:

> I believe that the day has come when we can combine sensory deprivation with drugs, hypnosis and astute manipulation of reward and punishment to gain almost absolute control over an individual's behavior. It should be possible then to achieve a very rapid and highly effective type of positive brainwashing that would allow us to make dramatic changes in a person's behavior and personality. I foresee the day when we could convert the worst criminal into a decent, respectable citizen in a matter of a few months—or perhaps even less time than that. . . .
>
> We must begin by drafting new laws that will be as consonant as possible with all the human-behavior data that scientists have gathered. We should try to

regulate human conduct by offering rewards for good behavior whenever possible instead of threatening punishment for breaches of the law. We should reshape our society so that we all would be trained from birth to do what society wants us to do. We have the techniques now to do it. Only by using them can we hope to maximize human potentiality. Of course, we cannot give up punishment entirely, but we can use it sparingly, intelligently, as a means of shaping people's behavior rather than as a means of releasing our own aggressive tendencies. For misdemeanors or minor offenses we would administer brief, painless punishment, sufficient to stamp out the antisocial behavior. We'd assume that a felony was clear evidence that the criminal had somehow acquired full-blown social neurosis and needed to be cured, not punished. We'd send him to a rehabilitation center where he'd undergo positive brainwashing until we were quite sure he had become a law-abiding citizen who would not again commit an antisocial act. We'd probably have to restructure his entire personality.[6]

I have described this statement as extreme, but it would be more accurate to call it a particularly blunt expression of values that are quite widely held. Rehabilitation is considered the most enlightened way of dealing with crime by a large and influential segment of the American bureaucracy, and such psychological rehabilitation centers as McConnell describes are already in existence.[7]

Another interesting sign of the politicization of psychology is a new movement calling itself radical therapy, which takes the position that the task of therapy must be social change and that any form of encouragement of adjustment is concealed social control:

> The therapist . . . allies himself to the status quo—and bolsters it. . . .
> Claiming to be "detached and clinical," therapists never are. They can't be. Their words and acts demonstrate their bias. Current therapy's emphasis on the individual cools people out and/or puts them down. It cools them out by turning their focus from society that fucks them over to own "hang-ups." It puts them down by making them "sick" people who need "treatment" rather than oppressed people who must be liberated.
> Therapy is change, not adjustment. This *means* change—social, personal, and political. When people are fucked over, people should help them fight it, and then deal with their feelings. A "struggle for mental health" is bullshit unless it involves changing this society which turns us into machines, alienates us from one another and our work, and binds us into racist, sexist and imperialist practices.[8]

It is characteristic that those who are farthest from the centers of power are most convinced that therapy is inherently political, while those who are in control usually maintain that it is not. Opponents of behaviorism charge that it is fascistic, but behaviorists insist that it is merely scientific. Radicals charge that establishment therapists are agents of the political power structure, but most therapists believe that they are merely helping people and that the therapeutic relationship has no political content whatever.

Because of this, it is quite difficult to get a clear picture of how different kinds of psychotherapy may affect the political awareness of those who undergo it. Arnold Rogow, a political scientist who made a survey of psychiatrists and Freudian analysts, found that most therapists insisted—no doubt correctly—that political subjects as such were seldom if ever discussed in therapy. But he also found that where patients do change their politics the shift is likely to be toward the center: "The consensus of both psychaitrists and psychoanalysts is that successful psychotherapy, by promoting open-mindedness, relative freedom from intrapsychic conflicts, and a decrease in rigidity of belief, moves patients toward a moderate or middle-road political position. . . . "[9] The most important thing about this, in my opinion, is its implicit assumption that improved mental health and middle-of-the-road politics naturally go together. This assumption is just the opposite of the "developmental radicalism" theory we discussed in the past chapter and of the therapeutic goals of such psychologists as Bugental, who hopes and believes that his patients are likely to emerge from therapy with a heightened awareness of the need for social change.[10]

There is a similar polarization, which has turned up at several points in this book, on the question of where in the social order one is most likely to encounter some form of pathology. Traditionally mental illness has been equated with social deviance. But such writers as Yablonsky, with his concept of robopathology, find the most dangerous sickness in the very essence of normal behavior.

This is not merely a theoretical issue, nor a concern of the psychiatric professionals alone. If, indeed, the act of diagnosing somebody as mentally ill is the first step toward changing the way that individual functions in society, then the extension of psychiatric surveillance into new areas is an extension of social control and a political issue. Ronald Leifer, a psychiatrist who is concerned about the underlying assumptions of "community psychiatry" and public "mental health" programs, writes:

As psychiatric services interlock with other community functions, increasing numbers of persons from every social class will come under psychiatric observation and influence—including growing numbers of former mental hospital patients, mental health clinic clients, welfare recipients, juvenile delinquents, criminals, employees of large corporations, members of the Armed Forces, and students, as well as the families of these persons. Under the guise of providing psychiatric diagnostic and treatment services, psychiatrists who are employed by public and private agencies may function as agents of social control, as personnel managers, and as promoters of the middle class ethic.[11]

This is another way of saying that there can be an enormous amount of political power concealed behind the supposedly neutral, objective, or scientific act of defining mental illness. And it is a power which can only be effectively exerted by those who already *have* power, as an extension of control over the relatively powerless. Dissenting psychologists can talk about pathology in the acts of leaders, but the leaders are not subsequently subject to the various acts of control—psychiatric diagnosis, behavior therapy, commitment—which are the fate of thousands of people at lower levels of society. Humanists can see pathology in institutions, but institutions do not get put away in hospitals. Leifer notes that "psychiatric power, as an instrument of the group, is particularly well suited for use against the individual. Since groups cannot be defined as mentally ill nor be committed, they are safe from psychiatric power."[12] I should make it clear, by the way, that the aim of the humanistic movement is not to get control of psychiatric power, or of the power to define who is "sick," but rather to do away with such power entirely. "The fundamental conflicts in human life," according to Szasz, "are not between competing ideas, one 'true' and the other 'false'—but rather between those who hold power and use it to oppress others and those who are oppressed by power and seek to free themselves of it."[13]

Most humanistic psychiatrists and psychologists prefer to steer clear of the medical model, in which an individual's total behavior is conceptualized in the same terms as physical illness, and opt for the growth model. Similarly most humanistic therapies strive to reduce the authoritarian character of the therapist—this is fundamental to Rogerian nondirectional counseling, to gestalt work in which the patients are expected to take responsibility for themselves, to encounter work in which the leader is also a participant. Many practitioners, in fact, refuse even to call their work "therapy" at all. Therapy means healing, healing implies sickness, and to be sick is to be powerless or less than fully responsible for oneself.

Once we admit of the idea of therapy as social control, and of any kind of "adjustment" therapy as a means of enforcement of the consciousness which the social system requires, then we must take a new look, not only at traditional ideas of "mental health" and "neurosis," but at madness as well. Schizophrenia, for example, is a concept which, although relatively new—it dates from the publication of Eugen Bleuler's monograph *La schizophrenie* in 1911—is widely accepted as a valid description of certain kinds of mental illness. Yet R. D. Laing argues that the concept of schizophrenia is at best a hypothesis, and furthermore that the behavior which the term is generally used to describe is, in a way, rational: "It seems to us that *without exception* the experience and behavior that gets labeled schizophrenic is a *special strategy that a person invents in order to live in an unlivable* situation."[14] The behavior so labeled is a way of dealing with society, and the label itself is a way society deals with certain individuals, rejects them, and strips them of their most basic human rights:

"Schizophrenia" is a diagnosis, a label applied by some people to others. This does not prove that the labeled person is subject to an essentially pathological process, of unknown nature and origin, going on *in* his or her body. It does not mean that the process is, primarily or secondarily, a *psycho-*pathological one, going on *in* the *psyche* of the person. But it does establish as a social fact that the person labeled is one of Them. It is easy to forget that the process is a hypothesis, to assume that it is a fact, then to pass the judgement that it is biologically maladaptive and, as such, pathological. But social adaptation to a dysfunctional society may be very dangerous. The perfectly adjusted bomber

pilot may be a greater threat to species survival than the hospitalized schizophrenic deluded that the Bomb is inside him. Our society may itself have become
biologically dysfunctional, and some forms of schizophrenic alienation of society
may have a sociobiological function that we have not recognized. . . .

There is no such "condition" as "schizophrenia," but the label is a social fact
and the social fact a *political event*. This political event, occurring in the civic order
of society, imposes definitions and consequences on the labeled person. It is a
social prescription that rationalizes a set of social actions whereby the labeled
person is annexed by others, who are legally sanctioned, medically empowered
and morally obliged, to become responsible for the person labeled. The person
labeled is inaugurated not only into a role, but into a career of patient, by the
concerted action of a coalition (a "conspiracy") of family, G.P., mental health
officer, psychiatrists, nurses, psychiatric social workers, and often fellow patients. The "committed" person labeled as patient, and specifically as "schizophrenic," is degraded from full existential and legal status as human agent and
responsible person to someone no longer in possession of his own definition of
himself, unable to retain his own possessions, precluded from the exercise of his
discretion as to whom he meets, what he does. His time is no longer his own and
the space he occupies is no longer of his choosing. After being subjected to a
degradation ceremonial known as psychiatric examination, he is bereft of his civil
liberties in being imprisoned in a total institution known as a "mental" hospital.
More completely, more radically than anywhere else in our society, he is
invalidated as a human being.[15]

The issue of civil rights is a particularly important one here. We
seldom take note of the fact that those individuals who do not participate
in the shared consciousness we define as sanity do not enjoy the
protections of citizenship. In America members of all the racial minority
groups, women, children, even convicted murderers, have legally
guaranteed rights that those who are defined as mentally ill do not. They
are the true outsiders. This situation might be tolerable if there were no
responsible differences of opinion whatever about what madness and
sanity really are. But since there is a great deal of difference of opinion,
and getting to be more all the time, the imprisonment and degradation of
thousands of people without due process of law must be questioned also.

Thomas Szasz, a psychiatrist who has been making himself unpopular
in his profession for more than a decade now, in a series of books whose
title convey the gist of his argument—*The Myth of Mental Illness, Law,
Liberty and Psychiatry, The Manufacture of Madness*—argues that the
existence of such a thing as "mental illness" has never been proved with
enough certainty to justify the enormous persecution of all those who
happen to get branded with such a designation. He considers the whole
institutionalized treatment of insanity to be a modern version of the
Inquisition: the age of science enforces its view of the world, as the age
of faith did; insanity replaces witchcraft:

What we call modern, dynamic psychiatry is neither a glamorous advance over
the superstitions and practices of the witch-hunts, as contemporary psychiatric
propagandists would have it, nor a retrogression from the humanism of the
Renaissance and the scientific spirit of the Enlightenment, as romantic tradition-

alists would have it. In actuality, Institutional Psychiatry is a continuation of the Inquisition. All that has really changed is the vocabulary and the social style. The vocabulary conforms to the intellectual expectations of our age: it is a pseudo-medical jargon that parodies the concepts of science. The social style conforms to the political expectations of our age: it is a pseudoliberal social movement that parodies the ideals of freedom and rationality.[16]

Szasz attaches a good deal of importance to the distinction between contractual psychotherapy—in which the patient voluntarily seeks treat-ment—and involuntary psychotherapy, in which the patient is submitted to treatment against his or her will. Much of the case of his criticism of the mental health policy of public agencies rests on the fact that such policies represent an enormous increase in the number of people exposed to some form of involuntary therapy.

I am not at all sure that a line can really be drawn between therapy which is voluntary or contractual and that which is involuntary. In penal institutions, for example, authorities insist that inmates are subjected to aversion therapy only with their consent. But the consent of a prison-er—who in our "enlightened" penal systems is likely to be serving an indeterminate sentence which means that his or her chances of being released are contingent upon "good" behavior—is quite meaningless. Outside of institutions, people who enter into contractual therapy are often under a great deal of social pressure to do so. People who voluntarily submit to aversion therapy for the treatment of alcoholism or deviant sexual behavior are faced with the alternative between "cure" and a wide range of social sanctions including criminal punishment. And people who receive psychotherapy within school systems or within the armed services, are quite likely to be under institutional pressure to do so. The more clearly involuntary the therapy is, the more likely that some form of behavior modification therapy is used. Behavior therapy, built upon a foundation of experimentation in techniques of control with laboratory animals, is the *only* kind of therapy which claims effectiveness with involuntary subjects.

Sanity and Citizenship

I have tried to indicate what some of the issues are, the political issues that are emerging as part of the political polarization in the psychologi-cal/psychiatric professions. I believe this polarization is increasing, and becoming more widely noticed. Consider the appearance of new books on the subject: *The Manufacture of Madness* in 1970, *The Politics of Therapy* and *The Radical Therapist* in 1971. I expect that the polarization will continue to increase, because I believe that the fundamental idea of sanity as adjustment, and the whole world-view which supports that idea, are being challenged.

The perspective outlined at the beginning of this chapter was a view of the political order as the visible, institutional superstructure of a shared consciousness—the enforcement of a general social consensus about what the world is like, what it means to be human, what the purposes and possibilities of life are. This world-view is generally described as secular, scientific, technological. It is causing the pollution of the planet, the murder and oppression of millions of people, and a diminution of the freedom and human potential of every single person who is subject to it.

One of the recurrent themes in humanistic psychology is the idea that a fundamental change in human consciousness, a new world-view, is emerging. Some people talk about a new paradigm; Maslow talks about a new Zeitgeist; Harman talks about a new Copernican revolution. Sometimes the change is defined in moral or behavioral terms: Bugental's humanistic ethic, Schutz's honesty revolution. Sometimes the language is loftier, and the perspective is cosmic. Alan Watts considers the human ego, by which he means the consciousness of oneself as a separate entity in and against the world, to be biologically maladaptive; for humanity to survive, that consciousness must change. The change means that human beings wake up to their membership in the universe; it also means that the universe wakes up to itself:

Is it entirely unreasonable to suppose that the situation may correct itself, that the "field pattern" man/universe may be intelligent enough to do so? If this happens, or is happening, it will at first appear that individuals are initiating the changes on their own. But as the required change takes place, the individuals involved will simultaneously undergo a change of consciousness revealing the illusion of their isolation.[17]

This last statement will probably strike many readers as a bit far-out. It should; it should seem at least as far-out as would have, at the comparable times, the idea that the earth is not the center of the solar system, that the human race has evolved from simpler species. An idea that does not seem far out has no right to be considered in any discussion of basic world-view.

It is not necessary, for the purposes of the point I am trying to make here, that the reader accept Watts' or anybody else's image of the cosmos. It is only necessary to accept the proposition that a rather widespread and meaningful dialogue on the subject is in progress. And if there exists any widespread difference of perspective on such profound and fundamental concepts, then it is inevitable that there would also be a difference of perspective on such relatively superficial matters as the meaning of sanity, and the best way for human beings to organize their societies.

From the perspective that I have been trying to outline—the idea of political institutions as the expressions of a shared consciousness or basic world-view—certain things which otherwise go unexplained begin to fit together and make sense. It is quite logical, for one thing, that people whose minds operate in a totally different way should be treated as sick and deprived of the rights of citizenship. They are, in a very real sense, not citizens; they are aliens (psychiatrists used to be called alienists), outside the community of rational beings. It is also logical that people who do not wish to share the prevailing world-view should try to renounce their citizenship in it, to "drop out," work "outside the system." The psychedelic battle cry of Timothy Leary—tune in, turn on, drop out—makes sense in an age when a significant number of people have come to see the state as a state of mind. And I personally see a good deal of logic in Leary's demand that he be regarded as a political prisoner.

I do not believe, by the way, that "dropping out" by some deliberate act of de-enculturation is at all easy; in fact it may not be possible at all. They used to say that you can take the boy out of the country but you can't take the country out of the boy. That sturdy Freudian garrison, the superego, is still standing in all of us, although a lot of people do appear to have it under pretty heavy siege. American values, sometimes in their best forms, sometimes in their worst, still provide form and structure to the lives of even the most dedicated dissidents. Part of the vast disillusionment that crept over the hippie movement had to do, I believe, with the gradual discovery that you could not step outside of American culture and make it go away.

Yet we have all around us the conviction that some form of de-enculturation is possible and desirable, and that conviction underlies most of the philosophies we have encountered in this book. Maslow describes superior people, self-actualized people, as individuals who have to some extent grown free of their culture. Gestalt therapists speak of a discovery of inner autonomy as a way of either keeping one's bearings in a time of vast cultural change or of preparing the way for a true revolution. Disciplines such as Zen describe the cultural world-view as an illusion, a kind of socially patterned dream from which every individual must strive to awaken. Hampden-Turner sees the transcendence of culture as the source of the most principled kind of political behavior. Laing calls the official world-view of Western society a kind of madness, perhaps more dangerous than the kind that is defined as such and treated in the mental hospitals.

I think that, rather than talk about people being in or out of the culture, in or out of the system, we would do well to step back a bit and see that in a very real sense everybody is in the culture and in the system. That's what makes it interesting—we are living in a culture which has evolved within itself a theory and practice of de-enculturation. And we are living within a political system which has conflict not only *for* power and *within* the rules but also conflict about what kind of power should exist (if any) and what kind of rules there ought to be (if any).

And when there are so many dissident voices, when even the most fundamental perceptions of reality and rationality are being challenged, there is inevitably pressure to reduce the range of choice, to create a somewhat more comfortably homogeneous society in which one may live out one's life without struggling with so many fearful uncertainties. Szasz calls attention to our need for a homogeneous society when he draws a parallel between the Inquisition and institutional psychiatry.

Each of them, he says, "tranquilizes the massive anxieties mobilized by what is generally experienced as an excess of choices. . . . " And this tranquilizing effort, he charges, is essentially totalitarian: "What these seemingly diverse 'therapeutic' movements have in common not only with one another but also with such modern totalitarian movements as National Socialism and Communism, is that each seeks to protect the integrity of an excessively heterogenous and pluralistic society and its dominant ethic."[18]

Let me return to my basic thesis that the changes and the dialogue that are going on in America today are enormous and profound, that they have to do with the most fundamental realities—ideas about what it means to be human. In this dialogue or process, everybody is changing: a field theory of human development means that every person is seen as an individual/environment gestalt. Nobody is standing still, because there is no still place to stand. However, the differences among individuals are enormous: personal development means not only a change of opinion, a change of *what* one thinks, but also a change of consciousness, a change of *how* one thinks.

One aspect of this dialogue has been the experimentation with, the interest in alternate life styles, alternative institutions. I expect that there will be a growing interest in alternative governments, more consideration of new and basically different ways of organizing human society.

Notes

[1] R. D. Laing, *The Politics of Experience* (London: Penguin Books Ltd.) © R. D. Laing, 1967. p. 81.
[2] Thomas Szasz, *The Manufacture of Madness* (New York: Delta, 1971), p. 58.
[3] Roszak, *The Making of a Counter Culture* (New York: Doubleday, 1969). Roszak's territory overlaps considerably with humanistic psychology: the five men he cites as chief theorists of the counterculture are two Freudian radicals (Norman O. Brown and Herbert Marcuse), two students of Eastern philosophy (Allen Ginsberg and Alan Watts), and one gestalt therapist (Paul Goodman).
[4] Seymour L. Halleck, *The Politics of Therapy* (New York: Science House, 1971), p. 11.
[5] *Ibid.*, p. 12.
[6] James V. McConnell, "Criminals Can Be Brainwashed—Now," Excerpted from *Psychology Today* magazine, April 1970. Copyright © Communications/Research/Machines, Inc. p. 74.
[7] See Bernard Weiner, "Prison Psychiatry: The Clockwork Cure," *The Nation*, 3 April 1972; also Jessica Mitford, "Kind and Usual Punishment in California," *The Atlantic Monthly*, March 1971.
[8] Michael Glenn, introduction to *The Radical Therapist* ed. Jerome Agel (New York: Ballantine, 1971), pp. x–xi.
[9] Rogow, *The Psychiatrists* (see ch. 2, fn. 27), p. 72.
[10] Bugental, *Challenges of Humanistic Psychology* (see ch. 1, fn. 16), p. 12.
[11] Leifer, *In the Name of Mental Health*, pp. 224–225.
[12] *Ibid.*, p. 228.
[13] Szasz, *Manufacture of Madness*, p. 63.
[14] Laing, *Politics of Experience*, pp. 78–79.
[15] *Ibid.*, pp. 82–84.
[16] *Manufacture of Madness*, p. 27.
[17] *Psychotherapy East and West*, p. 32.
[18] Szasz, *Manufacture of Madness*, pp. 58–59.

XI. Humanizing Technology

Ours is a progressively technical civilization. . . . It is a civilization committed to the quest for continually improved means to carelessly examined ends.

—Robert Merton[1]

But instead of being confined to a resentment that destroys life in the act of hurling defiance, we can now act upon the nature of the machine itself, and create another race of these creatures, more efficiently adapted to the environment and to the uses of life.

—Lewis Mumford[2]

One of the remarkable things about the nature of social conflict in our time is that we have conflict not only between groups of people, but between people and objects. One often hears references to the Luddites, the group of early nineteenth-century English workmen who expressed their anger at what was happening in their country by attacking factory machinery. And I have always thought there was something particularly significant in the terminology chosen by Mario Savio during the Berkeley Free Speech Movement in 1964:

> There is a time when the operation of the machine becomes so odious, makes you so sick at heart that you can't take part; you can't even tacitly take part, and you've got to put your bodies upon the levers, upon all the apparatus and you've got to make it stop.[3]

It does seem strange, in a way, that machine has become such an epithet in our language, that technology is so often seen as the natural enemy of human life—people created our machines, after all, and all of us enjoy and depend upon many of the benefits of technology. Yet there is a widespread fear that the machinery is out of control, that the massive technological system of which we are all a part has taken on a life of its own, is spinning mindlessly and destructively onward with no regard for human purpose, and is indeed forcing human beings to become increasingly machinelike themselves—adapting people to the service of the system.

I think that such fear is eminently well founded, but in this chapter I do not intend to present a case against technology. Rather, I want to examine technology from a humanistic perspective, and relate it to some of the political, psychological, and evolutionary concepts which we have previously explored. And I do not want to look at technology exclusively in terms of the crises it creates—overpopulation, pollution, etc.—but more fundamentally, in terms of its meaning and potential as a human tool.

114

I say *technology* but it would be as appropriate to use some term such as *technique*, in the way Jacques Ellul has used it—for we are dealing not merely with machines but with all the ways people organize action. Ellul writes:

The machine is not even the most important part of technique (although it is perhaps the most spectacular); technique has taken over all of man's activities, not just his production activity.

From another point of view, however, the machine is deeply symptomatic: it represents the ideal toward which technique strives. The machine is solely, exclusively, technique; it is pure technique, one might say. For, wherever a technical factor exists, it results, almost inevitably, in mechanization: technique transforms almost everything it touches into a machine.[4]

The process Ellul describes—motivated by the drive for greater efficiency, the urge to mechanize, what Lewis Mumford calls the will-to-order—is essentially the same thing as what Max Weber called rationalization. Weber saw this process at work in all areas of life: in the social sphere it produces bureaucracy. The bureaucratized organization—public agency, private corporation—is the social equivalent of the machine. Our social machines and our physical machines are produced out of the same basic human drive and shaped by the same cultural values, and the challenge they present—which is to design them to a human scale and suit them to human needs—although many sided, is one challenge. We have already discussed the encounter movement as, in part, an effort to humanize social machines; here we will be dealing mainly with physical machinery, with technology in the more common usage of the word.

In my opinion the best guide into this subject, certainly the writer who relates most closely to the humanistic movement in America, is Lewis Mumford. Almost all of his work has to do with the human potential, so to speak, of technology—with the prospects for the creative design and use of buildings and machines.

He is not among the technophobes. The machine, as he sees it, is ambivalent:

It is both an instrument of liberation and one of repression. It has economized human energy and it has misdirected it. It has created a wide framework of order and it has produced muddle and chaos. It has nobly served human purposes and it has distorted and denied them.[5]

Mumford refuses to concede that the technological drive is either inherently materialistic or tied to some urge to "dominate nature." Rather, he argues that the historical evidence as easily supports a view of it as a creative interaction of the human imagination with environmental conditions—creative in the sense that the drive is fundamentally an urge toward a continual re-creation of humanity itself. "Man is pre-eminently a mind-making, self-mastering, and self-designing animal," he writes. "I submit that at every stage man's inventions and transformations were less for the purpose of increasing the food supply or controlling nature than for utilizing his own immense organic resources and expressing his latent potentialities.''[6]

It is interesting, and characteristic of Mumford's perspective, that he cites the development of speech as the most significant early human technological achievement. This is seldom thought of as a *technological* development, but in Mumford's view it is precisely that. The development of speech requires the creative adaptation of a number of organs, each apparently evolved for other purposes, into a new mechanism which is not merely a tool but the agency of a total transformation of the human species:

The evolution of language—a culmination of man's more elementary forms of expressing and transmitting meaning—was incomparably more important to further human development than the chipping of a mountain of hand-axes. Beside the relatively simple coordination required for tool-using, the delicate interplay of many organs needed for the creation of articulate speech was a far more striking advance. This effort must have occupied a greater part of early man's time, energy, and mental activity, since the ultimate collective product, spoken language, was infinitely more complex and sophisticated at the dawn of civilization than the Egyptian or Mesopotamian kit of tools. [7]

Mumford's view, that the technological drive is inherently organic and life enhancing, sets him apart from such critics as Jacques Ellul, who stresses the tendency of technique to dehumanize wherever it appears. Although Mumford, as we will see, is very much a critic of the uses to which human inventiveness has been put in modern society, he insists that technology has, on the whole, been the vehicle of creative change, an integral part of human evolution:

The main business of man was his own self-transformation, group by group, region by region, culture by culture. This self-transformation not merely rescued man from permanent fixation in his original animal condition, but freed his best-developed organ, his brain, for other tasks than those of ensuring physical survival. The dominant human trait, central to all other traits, is this capacity for conscious, purposeful self-identification, self-transformation, and ultimately for self-understanding.

Every manifestation of human culture, from ritual and speech to costume and social organization, is directed ultimately to the remodelling of the human organism and the expression of the human personality. If it is only now that we belatedly recognize this distinctive feature, it is perhaps because there are widespread indications in contemporary art and politics and technics that man may be on the point of losing it—becoming not a lower animal, but a shapeless, amoeboid nonentity. [8]

The danger, in Mumford's opinion, arises from the misuse of technology due to a misunderstanding of its relationship to human needs. The evils which resulted from crash industrialization in the eighteenth and nineteenth centuries were the natural consequences of technology used according to a cultural value system which was disastrously shallow:

The important thing to bear in mind is that the failure to evaluate the machine and to integrate it in society as a whole was not due simply to defects in distributing income, to errors of management, to the greed and narrow-mindedness of the industrial leaders: it was also due to a weakness of the entire philosophy upon which the new techniques and inventions were grounded. The leaders and enterprisers of the period believed that they had avoided the necessity for introducing values, except those which were automatically recorded in profits and prices. They believed that the problem of justly distributing goods could be sidetracked by creating an abundance of them: that the problem of applying one's energies wisely could be cancelled out simply by multiplying them: in short, that most of the difficulties that had hitherto vexed mankind had a mathematical or mechanical—that is a quantitative—solution. The belief that values could be dispensed with constituted the new system of values.[9]

And Mumford's basic argument is that values cannot be dispensed with, that machinery is useful only insofar as it harmonizes with social purposes and human experiences:

Thus a steam turbine may contribute thousands of horsepower, and a speedboat may achieve speed: but these facts, which perhaps satisfy the engineer, do not necessarily integrate them in society. Railroads may be quicker than canalboats, and a gas-lamp may be brighter than a candle: but it is only in terms of human purpose and in relation to a human and social scheme of values that speed or brightness have any meaning. If one wishes to absorb the scenery, the slow motion of a canalboat may be preferable to the fast motion of a motor car. . . . [10]

This insistence that technology can and must be evaluated in terms of its contribution to human experience is fundamental to the humanistic perspective. Understanding this idea, we can begin to see how humanists may have something slightly different in mind when they employ such terms as "pollution," "environmental deterioration," or "ecological crisis." They are concerned not only with the physical, material, and quantifiable consequences of misuse of technology, but also with the emotional consequences. Thus the problem created by the automobile is not merely air pollution or driver safety, but also the total deprivation of any creative experience of work to which most of the people in automobile manufacture are subjected, the diminished experience of travel for the speeding passenger on an arrow-straight superhighway. The tragedy of mass merchandising is not only that so much merchandise is unsafe or defective, but that so many Americans experience most of their lives in the role of consumer.[11]

The situation can be conceptualized in terms of Maslow's need hierarchy. We have tended to utilize our technology toward the quantifiable satisfaction of the lower needs (food, shelter, etc.) and we recognize that things have gone wrong when the continued satisfaction of lower needs seems in doubt, when pollution threatens the physical health of the species. We are much less likely to think about using technology toward the satisfaction of higher needs (love, belongingness, self-actualization), and we are also less likely to recognize obstructions to higher-need gratification which have been caused by technological processes. This is because our cultural order, our collective conception of human experience, our social sciences such as economics and psychology which define the nature of human needs—all the things that, taken together, I have referred to as the established consciousness—tend to deny or de-emphasize higher needs.

I fear that when higher needs are recognized, it is often so that they may be manipulated. Prestige is often a factor in the merchandising of cars and homes, for example, but there is no serious attempt to understand the exteem needs of consumers and find the best way to satisfy them. The need to love and be loved is exploited by everybody from political candidates to toothpaste manufacturers, but any proposal to recognize this need and make its gratification a social goal would be considered laughable.

The task of articulating a new vision of human purpose, of adapting technology more suitably to human needs, is inevitably political. Although some facets of humanistic psychology—especially the encounter-group movement—seem to be a move toward decentralization, toward social organizations on a more human (i.e., smaller) scale, there is at the same time a fairly general recognition of the need for some forms of large, even worldwide social organization. Mumford notes:

> The machine imposes the necessity for collective effort and widens its range. To the extent that men have escaped the control of nature they must submit to the control of society. As in a serial operation every part must function smoothly and be geared to the right speed in order to ensure the effective working of the process as a whole, so in society at large there must be a close articulation between all of its elements. Individual self-sufficiency is another way of saying technological crudeness: as our technics becomes more refined it becomes impossible to work the machine without large-scale collective cooperation, and in the long run a high technics is possible only on a basis of worldwide trade and intellectual intercourse.[12]

The new awareness of ecology which has begun to dawn upon most of us in recent years shows us another reason why technology necessitates some forms of worldwide social organization. We have been finding out that technical processes which we had formerly believed to be more or less isolated and localized—pesticide use, power production, mining, many kinds of industry—have in fact far-reaching and complex effects upon nature. Technology lends a formidable reality to the somewhat idealistic notion of the world as a single ecosystem; our machinery may succeed, where a host of religions and ideologies have failed, in forcing us all to recognize the need for a human community.

The age of ecological politics has barely begun, but it is already apparent that politics has become chiefly a matter of making decisions about how to use technology. A considerable body of anthropologists, historians, and political theorists (Marx among them) would argue that it has always been that. Certainly it is that now. This fact is most obvious in the case of the issues we call ecological but it is equally true of most major political issues. Defense, farm, and economic policies, all are matters of the proper uses of technology as matters of public decision-making.

Now there is a strong urge, which has deep roots in our cultural value system, to leave decisions about the proper use of technology to the experts. This urge drives us toward the kind of social order which is described, quite accurately, as technocratic.

Yet there stands against the drift toward a technocratic society a considerable body of opinion that the experts—at any rate the kind of experts our social and educational system seems to produce—are precisely the *least* qualified people to make decisions about how technology should be used. Hampden-Turner's researches put scientists and technologists fairly low on the list of occupational groups showing any potential for enlightened leadership. He cites research finding that engineering students, in comparison with other student groups, were "uncreative, unimaginative, narrow minded, materialistic, security seeking, prestige oriented, parochial, authoritarian, ultra-masculine, anti-intellectual, and unable or unwilling to play a part in university controversies and affairs."[13] Hardly an encouraging prospect for a technocratic Brave New World, yet the fact remains that a substantial portion of public policy is shaped by engineers. The great national orgy of paving and dam building which has taken place over the past couple of decades is evidence of this kind of technocracy at work.

The weakness of technocracy is not merely in the lack of social vision of many people who hold power; it is a weakness of the systems themselves, of the kinds of thought and action that the bureaucratic organizations of a technological society seem to produce. One of the characteristics of a technical civilization is the proliferation of specialties. Areas of knowledge and action become compartmentalized, divide into still smaller compartments, become more sealed off from one another as data increases; special languages, sometimes incomprehensible to outsiders, come into use within each area of specialization. Courses of action are then pursued according to the drives which emanate from within the specialty; things are done not because there is a universal need for them, but because the "state of the art" has made them possible.

People within a specialty develop a passionate and sincere conviction that whatever it is they do (whether they are an agency, a company, or an academic discipline) must be done. This narrowing is in large part the result of socialization: people become so identified with the part of the system within which they work, so identified with their special roles in it, that they tend to lose their sense of membership in other communities, in society, or the human race. I have argued elsewhere[14] that this process not only creates problems but also makes it more difficult to solve them; the same limited vision, which has precipitated a number of ecological crises, can be found among those people whom we expect to understand the nature of ecological crisis and to devise solutions.

The recent wave of ecological political controversy is in part a revolt against technocracy itself: every issue of this kind represents an effort to take some aspect of policy away from technocratic decision-making agencies and bring it into the area of public politics. So far the task for the environmentalists and conservationists has been rendered rather difficult by the fact that the policy questions they want to debate have already been turned into *faits accomplis* by the technocrats. The typical environmental controversy is a situation in which environmentalists call attention to some action, plan, policy, or project which has been developed quietly by technologists and bureaucrats, usually with little or no public discussion. The work of the environmentalists is to create public discussion where there was none before, to make political issues out of matters previously classified as nonpolitical.

Because they have so often been trying to call a halt to projects already in motion, the environmentalists have unfortunately acquired a somewhat Luddite character in the opinion of many people; because they so often oppose the way technology is used, they seem to be against technology itself. And undoubtedly there are many people in the environmental movement who *are* against technology, who see human inventiveness and the machinery it creates as their natural enemies. But I think the time will come when it will be possible for environmentalists to think of *using* technology in the service of ecological sanity, when their task will be not only to stop projects but also to inaugurate them.

Ecology, I believe, is not merely a new issue, it is a new kind of issue. Ecological politics opens up for us the fundamental question of how a technological society is to be run, whether technology must inevitably lead to technocracy. It forces us to consider the possibilities of a technological democracy, to envision the time when the major issues of technological planning will be articulated by political leaders and will be dealt with openly as the critical questions of public policy which they have always been anyway.

As this happens, we are confronted with the realization that our level of technological achievement does not relieve us of the necessity for thinking about what we want to be and do. Technology does not just open up before us a single road, a straight line toward more of everything, toward some day of quantitative triumph when every man, woman, and child in America has two cars and every hungry foreigner can be given a freezer full of TV dinners. Rather, it opens up a bewildering variety of choices and possibilities. It challenges us to comprehend what the alternatives available to us are, and to find ways to pursue them and make the pursuit an integral part of our social purposes and human existence. And consequently we have to think about what our social purposes are, what human existence is and may become. It means that we have to deal in political terms with the same enormous questions that have launched the movement described in these pages as humanistic psychology.

The basic question is, can a highly technological society at the same time be democratic and aimed at the continuing development of all people—in Mumford's words, "self-knowledge, self-government, and self-actualization"[15]? The difficulties in the way of such an achievement are great, because technology has shown a tremendous capacity to regiment and alienate people, to centralize (big government, big business, big labor, mass media), to specialize fields of knowledge, to narrow the range of discourse on fundamental questions, and to lull us all into giving up our control of the machinery in return for the satisfactions of the consumer's life. According to Ellul, technique does all these things without plan: there are no conspirators, only inexorable "laws of development" which determine what a technological society *must* become. I do not personally believe that these "laws" are irreversible, but I do think that it is necessary to understand them—to recognize that they are real and powerful tendencies in the technological process—in order to control them; awareness is change.

And for a technological democracy to function, a high level of public awareness is necessary. This kind of awareness is not needed in a technocracy, which can function at peak efficiency with a minimal level of public awareness of what is going on, all decisions made by the specialists right up to the moment it destroys itself. A technological democracy—which is the kind of political system I confidently believe we are developing—requires an extremely high level of awareness on the part of all its citizens. It requires that we move in our technologized world environment with the same skill, sureness, and sense of harmony with which Eskimos learned to function in the forbidding snow and ice, and with which Polynesian tribes performed their incredible feats of navigation. I mention these adaptive successes here because they are evidence that ordinary human beings have an enormous capacity for comprehending the nature of an environment and living in it richly and creatively.

By awareness I mean several things: one aspect of awareness is the kind we understand best, scientific knowledge; obviously, if we are to make rational decisions about the uses of technology, we must have sophisticated information about it, widely distributed. We need to know, for example, the consequences of using different kinds of pesticides. Another aspect of awareness is the sense of oneself; people need to have a greater respect for, and sensitivity toward, what is going on inside them emotionally and physically, how they really feel and what they really want. Another is the awareness of the environment, the sense of being a real and inseparable part of the human race and the physical universe; this kind of awareness, we are learning, can be highly developed in some individuals, in some cultures, and almost totally lost in others. These kinds of awareness are separable conceptually but not in reality; the development of one at the expense of others is not the development of a whole person, and whole people are the only kind who are likely to survive.

Evidence of Positive Changes

I suspect that this discussion may sound rather idealistic and philosophical; people are going to have to get better. To make the discussion more concrete I would like to cite here a number of different things which are, to me, evidence that a lot of people are working hard at developing the kind of awareness which is necessary if we are to wake up and take control of the machinery.

1. Environmental Politics

The increased public concern with environmental issues, the growth of such groups as the Sierra Club, Friends of the Earth, and Zero Population Growth, is raising basic questions about technological policy, challenging decisions made by technocratic fiat. Environmentalists have of necessity tended to emphasize survival issues, but they have also raised questions of aesthetics, higher needs, human experience, and the integration of technology with social purpose, and have opened up new dialogue about the nature of the human race and its relation to world ecology. The movement has also produced a spurt of new periodicals and books devoted to ecology and environmental politics, and has helped to stimulate new theoretical work on ecology.

2. Ecological Life Style

Closely related to the above, this phenomenon involves the various efforts of many people to make some changes in their living habits toward improved personal health and a more harmonious relationship to the environment. The organic-food boom is perhaps the most conspicuous example of this phenomenon, but by no means the whole thing; one can get a feel for the mystique of this movement by leafing through the pages of *The Last Whole Earth Catalog*. It is, I think, significant that the catalog (subtitled *Access to Tools*) is heavily oriented toward the acquisition of technological skills and scientific understanding as part of personal development and everyday life. Among the "tools" offered in the catalog are two books by Lewis Mumford and several by Buckminster Fuller.

3. Consciousness-raising

I believe this term originated with the women's liberation movement rather than with some school of therapy. It doesn't matter, because liberation and growth overlap; while the emphasis may be personal for some and political for others, it can never be exclusively one or the other. Any process that develops the awareness of individuals—puts them in greater touch with their own feelings and experiences, gives them a clearer sense of what they do and how they are done to—is a force for both personal development and political change. People who begin to take responsibility for themselves, to seek freedom and dignity on their own terms, are not easily regimented into technocratic systems.

4. The Consumer Movement

Because the very essence of technocratic regimentation is the willingness of the masses to function mainly as consumers, it is an event of great political moment when the consumers begin to act up. And it does appear that a considerable number of people are experiencing a certain kind of consciousness-raising in this respect, beginning to pay greater attention to the nature of the things they buy and use, struggling to assume a more active part in this system and to make it more responsive to their own needs. Closely related to this change is the recent resurgence of investigative reporting, of the kind that used to be called muckraking, about the practices of corporations and public agencies. The key figure in this field is Ralph Nader, whom I personally consider to be one of our best political scientists. It is particularly important to note, in relation to the technocracy-vs.-technological-democracy distinction I have been trying to make here, that Nader's research findings are not produced for a narrow circle of academic specialists but for the public; their purpose is to increase public awareness of how the machinery actually functions.

The Four Movements in Perspective

I am quite aware of the fact that the four movements I have mentioned would not be conceded by everybody—including some of their leaders—to be parts of the same larger historical process. But it is my own conviction that they are and that, furthermore, it would be quite possible to view the process from an even wider angle, and to see as part of it a number of other apparently unrelated social phenomena including the civil rights movement, the popularization of Oriental philosophies, the various neo-Reichian "body" therapies, and the sexual freedom movement. Theordore Roszak, in his introduction to a recent anthology, conceptualizes liberation in terms of five concentric circles: person, body, community, whole earth, transcendence. [16] Which is about as wide a perspective on the subject as you can get.

Although we are dealing here with a major area of the history of Western civilization, and with a vast and varied stirring of responses to it, the general point of view which I have been trying to communicate can be fairly simply summarized: technological development does contain strong dehumanizing, materialistic forces, and it does tend to pressure human beings to forego and forget their own needs and adjust themselves to the needs of systems. But if people can get in touch with their own needs and fight for them, if scientists can help them by making human needs and human growth a central object of their study, and if political leaders can honestly and imaginatively present technological alternatives as public issues—then there is the possibility that technology can become truly the servant of human needs, and that furthermore we can use it creatively to transform ourselves and our society.

Bio-Feedback

I want to mention here one specific area of scientific research (and technological application) which I believe will add a certain depth of meaning to some of the things we have just been discussing: namely, bio-feedback research, the most significant body of experimental or laboratory work identified with humanistic psychology.

Up to this point I have probably conveyed the impression that the humanistic movement is entirely the product of theoreticians and clinical psychologists. It is true that this kind of work makes up the great majority of third force psychology, but not all of it. The experimental work of such researchers as Elmer and Alyce Green of the Menninger Foundation in Topeka, Joe Kamiya and Robert Ornstein of the Langley Porter Neuropsychiatric Institute in San Francisco and Stanley Krippner of the Maimonides Medical Center in Brooklyn is an important part of humanistic psychology. Their work tends to be explorations of consciousness and the possibilities of expanded mental functioning—they have studied dreams, hypnosis, altered states of consciousness, parapsychological phenomena, and the psychedelics.

Several researchers have studied the peculiar abilities of practitioners of such disciplines as Zen and Yoga. A handy way to tell a behavioristic experimental psychologist from a humanistic experimental psychologist is to check and see whether the instruments are connected to a rat or to a Zen master. The difference is a matter of basic orientation: behaviorist psychology operates on the assumption that laws generated from experimentation with simpler species can be applied to human behavior. Humanists study the most advanced accomplishments of individual men and women with the hope of opening up new possibilities of development for everybody else.

Zen, being concerned with techniques of concentration, produces people who have a high ability to control their own brain-wave patterns. Yoga, which also involves a complex system of physical exercises, apparently produces people who can control "involuntary" physiological processes such as heart rate. There have been medical reports of such phenomena from English physicians serving in India over the past two hundred years and some published papers by Indian psychologists. But Western psychologists have not paid attention to whether the claims of Yogis might have any basis in fact, nor have they considered the implications for the human species as a whole.

Recently some American psychologists have begun to study these phenomena with the most modern measuring techniques. Elmer Green at the Menninger Foundation psychophysiology lab in Topeka conducted a number of experiments with one Yogi and reported that the Yogi was able to control his heartbeat rate and blood pressure, produce a variety of brain-wave patterns at will, go to sleep voluntarily, and create a ten-degree temperature change in his hand in ten minutes.[17]

These abilities are developed by the Yogis, if at all, only after long years of intensive work. The researchers are now attempting to develop new and faster methods that enable people to develop increased control of physiological processes.

One early endeavor in this direction was the approach called autogenic training, developed early in this century by Johannes Schultz; this approach, involving a variety of techniques including self-hypnosis, aimed to teach individuals to learn to exercise some degree of control over specific physical functions, usually for medical or psychotherapeutic purposes.[18] Although the method had some success it also took a good deal of time for patients to get significant results, and autogenic training was never widely taken up in the United States. The form of training that *now* receives a good deal of attention is autogenic feedback training or bio-feedback; the difference between the older and the newer forms of training is the addition of sophisticated technology that enables the subject to know what the body is doing. With this kind of information— usually in the form of visual or auditory signals which give the subject data on the current heartbeat, brain waves, skin temperature and so forth—training appears to proceed at a much more rapid rate.

Bio-feedback work is still in its infancy, but it has already produced some valuable medical results. Green has found that most people can learn to influence their heart rate, skin temperature, and blood flow; further, he has found that learning blood-flow control produces a high rate of relief from migraine headache. Other researchers have worked with heart patients, individuals with high blood pressure, and various gastrointestinal ailments.[19] Bio-feedback also has great promise of developing ways to train intellectual and creative abilities, because individuals learn to put themselves into specific states of mind suitable to specific tasks. The aim here is to make scientifically definable and more widely accessible the states of consciousness, the peculiar cognitive skills of artists, scientists, and inventors. Some bio-feedback researchers have already suggested that bio-feedback education should train, from an early age, the control of bodily processes and states of consciousness.[20]

Bio-feedback is so promising, in fact, that many of the scientists associated with it seem to spend a good deal of their time either talking about its promise or warning the lay public against becoming too enthusiastic about it until the experimental results are more conclusive. Yet it has already begun to receive an enormous amount of public attention, for obvious reasons, and I am sure that the brief summary of research I have given above will not be received as news by many of the readers of this book. I have included it here because there are a couple of things about bio-feedback which are particularly significant:

1. It Is Voluntary

Although there has been some bio-feedback research with animals (and, to a lesser extent, with humans) using positive and negative reinforcements on the behaviorist model, most bio-feedback training is voluntary, in two senses of the world: it does not attempt to condition the subject through the use of punishment or reward, and it does attempt to give the subject voluntary control over responses previously believed to be involuntary. It is literally an expansion of consciousness, of the subject's awareness and self-control. A strict behaviorist could argue (as many have) that there are various positive reinforcements (such as approval) built into the bio-feedback training process. I would accept this argument as a hypothesis of equal value to the humanistic hypothesis that people strive naturally toward greater awareness and autonomy: "Voluntary control moves toward increased inner freedom; conditioned control moves toward loss of inner freedom."[21]

2. It Is Technological

Even the early forerunners of bio-feedback training—Zen, Yoga, autogenic training—were technological in the wider meaning of the word advocated by Mumford. And modern bio-feedback, with its vast repertoire of electronic devices, is certainly technological in the customary Western usage. In either case, it is a kind of technology which in a remarkable way supports Mumford's view of humanity as a mind-making, self-mastering, and self-designing animal, his view of the technological drive as aimed toward utilizing our organic resources and expressing latent potentialities. The aim of bio-feedback work appears to be to use the machinery to increase the capacities, the autonomy, and the freedom of human beings; to increase their range of choices, not to reduce them; to make the machine the servant of people, and not the reverse. Bio-feedback is only a fragment among the possibilities of a humanized technology but it illustrates particularly well how technology can be an organic agent of evolutionary change and not merely a mindless proliferation of junk.

Notes

[1] Robert Merton, foreword to Jacques Ellul, *The Technological Society* (New York: Alfred A. Knopf, Inc. 1964), p. vi.

[2] From *Technics and Civilization* by Lewis Mumford, copyright 1934, by Harcourt, Brace, Jovanovich, Inc.; renewed, 1962, by Lewis Mumford. Reprinted by permission of the publishers and Rutledge & Kegan Paul Ltd.

[3] See Sol Stern, "A Deeper Disenchantment" in *The Age of Protest*, (Pacific Palisades: Goodyear, 1969) ed. Walt Anderson, p. 61–62.

[4] Ellul, *The Technological Society*, p. 4.

[5] *Technics and Civilization*, p. 283.

[6] Mumford, *The Myth of the Machine: Technics and Human Development* (New York: Harcourt, Brace Jovanovich, Inc. and Martin Secker & Warburg Ltd. 1967), pp. 8–9.

[7] *Ibid.*, p. 8.

[8] *Ibid.*, p. 10.

[9] *Technics and Civilization*, p. 283.

[10] *Ibid.*, p. 282.

[11] A particularly valuable and important work in relation to American consumer culture, and the socialization of people into the consumer role, is Jules Henry, *Culture against Man* (New York: Random House, 1963).

[12] *Technics and Civilization*, p. 280.

[13] *Radical Man*, pp. 401–2.

[14] See introduction to Anderson, ed., *Politics and Environment: A Reader in Ecological Crisis* (Pacific Palisades, Calif.: Goodyear, 1970).

[15] Mumford, *The City in History* (New York: Harcourt, Brace Jovanovich, 1961) p. 573.

[16] Roszak, *Sources: An Anthology of Contemporary Materials Useful for Preserving Sanity While Braving the Great Technological Wilderness* (New York: Harper and Row, 1972).

[17] Elmer E. Green, "Biofeedback Training and Yoga," paper presented at Association for Humanistic Psychology conference on Psychic Healing, San Francisco, May 1972.

[18] J. H. Schultz and W. Luthe, *Autogenic Training: A Physiologic Approach in Psychotherapy* (New York: Grune and Stratton, 1959).

[19] Barnard Law Collier, "Brain Power: The Case for Bio-Feedback Training," *Saturday Review*, 10 April 1971.

[20] Richard Davidson and Stanley Krippner, "Bio-Feedback Research: The Data and Their Implications," paper presented at Second International Invitational Conference on Humanistic Psychology, July 21–24, University of Wurzburg, Germany, and at Seventeenth International Conference of Applied Parapsychology, July 25–30, 1971, Liège, Belgium.

[21] Elmer E. Green, Alyce M. Green, E. Dale Walters, "Voluntary Control of Internal States: Psychological and Physiological," *Journal of Transpersonal Psychology*, Spring 1970, p. 17. Reprinted by permission of the Transpersonal Institute, 2637 Marshall Drive, Palo Alto, California 94303.

XII. Education As Growth

"Right answers," specialization, standardization, narrow competition, eager acquisition, aggression, detachment from the self. Without them, it has seemed, the social machinery would break down. Do not call the schools cruel or unnatural for furthering what society has demanded. The reason we now need radical reform in education is that society's demands are changing radically. It is quite safe to say that the human characteristics now being inculcated will not work much longer. Already they are not only inappropriate, but destructive.

—George B. Leonard[1]

All the following fit together: Carl Rogers' insistence that the course of therapy must be charted by the client, not the therapist; Maslow's belief in the inner biological drive toward self-actualization; the Gestaltists' conviction that the development of personal awareness and responsibility enables individuals to change and move through their impasses; the encounter movement's confidence in group interaction as a way of developing the autonomy, openness, and spontaneity of individuals. These things add up to a general perspective on human growth, a consensus that it is natural for people to develop and change and reach out, and that while it is important that we recognize this and learn to help the process along, it can never be *done for* someone else. This perspective is, of course, as applicable to education as to therapy, and there is a growing body of work now available which outlines a humanistic approach to education.

We cannot go very far in the enterprise of creating a humanistic approach to politics unless we understand something of the humanistic approach to education; the present structure of our institutions is too inhibiting. And education is relevant to the field of politics for other reasons: (1) education is one of the chief concerns of modern governments—local, state, and, increasingly, national. (2) The educational policies we formulate today can have an enormous effect on the kind of society we have tomorrow, on the course of development of the human species.

It is a rather amazing fact, which seems stranger to me the more I think about it, that so little attention is paid in most academic disciplines—outside the field of education itself—to the question of how people learn. It is generally assumed, in the training of college-level faculty, that if one learns "the subject" he or she is then qualified to go forth and "teach" it to others. One cannot, in most states, become accredited as an elementary school teacher without some courses in education itself, but it is quite possible to become a professor, chairman of a department, even president of a university, without ever having been required to think seriously, in any fundamental way, about what learning *is*.

I am not advocating that political science graduate students be required to take education courses. That wouldn't help; most education departments are awash with behavior mod, and the prospective professor would probably just be trained in reinforcement techniques to make students shape up and learn their statistics. I am advocating, rather, that people who are to become college faculty be allowed to consider alternative ways of education. Alternatives do exist, and there are many responsible people who think that the way colleges and universities now operate is not the last word in human learning.

The fact that education is seldom taught or discussed as a subject in our academic disciplines does not mean that a theory of education does not exist and serve as a guide to them. On the contrary, there is a quite elaborate and complete theory of education; it so pervades the experience of students that they do not need to be taught it.

Carl Rogers has spelled out some of the implicit assumptions of this theory in a discussion of graduate education in psychology. I will summarize them here:

1: *The student cannot be trusted to pursue his own scientific and professional learning.* . . . It is almost uniformly true that the faculty attitude is one of mistrustful guidance. Work must be assigned, the completion of this work must be supervised; students must be continually guided and then evaluated. . . .

2: *Ability to pass examinations is the best criterion for student selection and for judging professional promise.* . . .

3: *Evaluation is education; education is evaluation.* . . . It is difficult to exaggerate the damage done to promising graduate students by this completely fallacious assumption that they learn by being threatened, time after time, with catastrophic failure. While I am sure that most faculty members would deny that they hold to this assumption, their behavior shows all too clearly that this is the operational principle by which they work.

4: *Presentation equals learning: What is presented in the lecture is what the student learns.* It scarcely seems possible that intelligent men could hold to this assumption. Yet one has only to observe a hard-working, serious-minded committee of faculty members arguing over the topics to be included in a graduate survey course in psychology to realize that in their view of the course, what is "covered" (a marvelous term!) is what is learned. . . .

5: *Knowledge is the accumulation of brick upon brick of content and information.* One might think that psychology, of all the scientific disciplines, would be the least likely to hold this implicit assumption. It is psychologists who have shown that learning takes place primarily and significantly when it is directly related to the meaningful purposes and motives of the individual. Yet most graduate departments proceed upon the conviction that there are a series of fundamental building blocks in the science of psychology which must be mastered sequentially by the student, whether or not they fit in with his current interests. . . .

6: *The truths of psychology are known.* . . . Often faculty members talk critically about dogmatism, yet display an extreme degree of it in their behavior.

Sometimes the orthodoxy is in regard to method, and it is the "truth methods" of scientific psychology that are regarded as immutable.

7: *Method is science. . . .* A rigorous procedure is often considered (if one may judge by faculty behavior) as far more important than the ideas it is intended to investigate. A meticulous statistics and a sophisticated research design seem to carry more weight than significant observations of significant problems. . . .

8: *Creative scientists develop from passive learners. . . .*

9: *"Weeding out" a majority of the students is a satisfactory method of producing scientists and clinicians. . . .* In some departments only one out of five, or even one out of seven of those who start actually obtain the degree. Usually this is regarded as evidence that the department maintains "high standards." . . . In my opinion, every student who leaves a department should be considered as a possible failure on the part of the department. . . .

10: *Students are best regarded as manipulable objects, not as persons. . . .* The current ultrabehavioristic philosophy which underlies today's psychology tends to see all individuals simply as machines, managed by reward and punishment. . . . Another factor . . . is that it is almost impossible to be close to a student if one's primary relationship to him is that of a judge and evaluator. [2]

These points are all about the education of psychologists but I believe that the same implicit assumptions, the same theory of education, can be found behind the other social sciences as well. In regard to political science, I would be inclined to amend one of Rogers' statements, number 6, to read as follows:

There is a great deal that is yet to be learned about politics, but we know how to go about learning it.[3]

I would also want to add to Rogers' list two more implicit assumptions:

1: *Research and learning is helped by dividing fields of knowledge into academic disciplines.*

2: *Boredom is an unavoidable part of the learning process, especially when one is dealing with important and complex subjects.*

It is, as Rogers notes, rather ironic that psychology departments, whose faculty are most likely to be aware of the rather enormous body of evidence tending to *refute* these implicit assumptions, continue to teach in the same way. It may be ironic, but it is quite understandable. The implicit assumptions continue to guide higher education for two main reasons: (1) they represent prevailing cultural values—the way most of us have been taught and the expectations most people have about what education should be. (2) They make the system work; they perpetuate the educational technocracy.

An alternative to the theory of education which we have been discussing has arisen in the past few years, a quite different view of how and why people learn. Like many of the things which I have presented in this book, this alternative is both a social movement and a coalescing body of theory and research; the most visible part of the movement, though not all of it, is the "free schools" movement. The educational theory which comes with it is closely involved with humanistic psychology—Rogers, Maslow, Perls, etc. Among the people who have written in this field are John Holt, Jonathan Kozol, Herbert Kohl, George Leonard, George Brown, and Paul Goodman.

An Alternative Way To Learn

I am going to try to state the salient points of this alternate theory of learning, and will amplify it here and there with references to various aspects of humanistic psychology. The main points, as I see them, are these:

1. *Human beings have a natural tendency to learn.* This might best be described, like self-actualization, as an inherent biological capacity. Learning is in some way relevant to every one of the human needs cited by Maslow, including the highest. Rogers believes that this potentiality for learning "is a tendency which can be trusted, and the whole approach to education (can be built) upon and around the student's natural desire to learn."[4]

2. *The learning process is a part of personal growth.* It involves not merely the acquisition of facts or data, but the continual reintegration of the individual with changes in self-image, feeling, behavior, relation to environment. This principle is holistic; it asserts that acquired knowledge has value only insofar as it is integrated with the individual's total development, and that evaluations of acquired knowledge, tests, are relatively meaningless when they do not take into account the needs, interests, plans, activities and environment of the people being evaluated.

George Brown, who is a professor of education at the University of California at Santa Barbara and a gestalt therapist, advocates "confluent education"—programs in which the relationship between feeling and thinking is fully recognized. Brown writes:

The position of most educators at all levels is that the primary function of schools is to teach the learner to be intellectually competent. The position is described by those who hold it as realistic, hardheaded, and a number of other fine-sounding things. Our belief is that this position is instead most unrealistic and illusionary. Oh, yes, it would greatly simplify matters if we could somehow isolate intellectual experience from emotional experience, but at the moment this is possible only in textbooks and experimental designs. The cold, hard, stubborn reality is that whenever one learns intellectually, there is an inseparable accompanying emotional dimension. The relationship between intellect and affect is indestructably symbiotic.[5]

3. *Conditions that facilitate personal growth facilitate learning. Conversely, conditions that inhibit personal growth inhibit learning.* In the most general terms, conditions that facilitate personal growth may be described as those which are nonthreatening, nourishing, open, flexible, stimulating.

Rogers notes that extreme difficulty is likely to be experienced by people who have reached a point at which some fundamental change in self-organization—in whom or what one believes oneself to be—seems necessary. This point is the personal equivalent of what happens to scientists when confronted with information that does not fit the present paradigm; it is a point of stress, and some people may be unable to pass through it; they will tend to resist acquiring the new information, because to acquire it means to change. A supportive environment, which encourages people to learn to trust their inner resources and take risks, makes change and learning easier; an environment which threatens people or which subjects them to ridicule and increases fear of failure, will obstruct the natural learning process.

Since learning is merely one facet of the urge toward self-actualization, we can correlate humanistic learning theory to Maslow's hierarchy of needs. This theory concedes that learning *can* be a response to threat, particularly when people are dealing with lower needs: threatened with starvation, people learn to hunt; threatened with exposure to the elements, they learn to build shelters; this might be called deficiency-motivated learning. But learning in response to threat is not all of learning: there is also being-motivated learning, which encompasses all the new things people will take in as they develop, as basic needs are taken care of and higher needs naturally emerge. This learning is not in response to threat, but in response to individual potentiality for growth. And the person who has best taken care of the basic security and self-esteem needs will be less threatened by new things, will be less anxious about maintaining an old self-image and thus most capable of changing in profound ways—literally reorganizing the self—when he or she recognizes that it is time to do so.

4. *When a person is ready to learn, knowledge will be easily assimilated; when a person is not ready, knowledge will be acquired with difficulty and probably not retained.* A person is "ready" to learn a given subject matter when his or her personal life-situation and developing needs make that subject necessary. When information becomes necessary to a person it also becomes interesting and suddenly quite learnable. Rogers puts it this way: "When an individual has a goal he wishes to achieve and he sees the material available to him as relevant to achieving that goal, learning takes place with great rapidity." [6] This seems such a simple, common-sense principle—and is so strongly validated besides by empirical research about learning—that it is truly amazing to consider how much of the educational system, from kindergarten to graduate school, is a systematic violation of it.

Testing is an integral part of this kind of education; indeed, I would say that the greater part of the things one learns in the course of progressing through the educational system are learned mainly for the purpose of taking examinations. It is also interesting to note how much of teaching is for the purpose of giving students material to pass examinations with. John Holt writes:

It begins to look as if the test-examination-marks business is a gigantic racket, the purpose of which is to enable students, teachers, and schools to take part in a joint pretense that the students know everything they are supposed to know, when in fact they know only a small part of it—if any at all. Why do we always announce examinations in advance, if not to give students a chance to cram for them? Why do teachers, even in graduate schools, always say quite specifically what the exam will be about, even telling the type of questions that will be given? Because otherwise too many students would flunk. What would happen at Harvard or Yale if a prof gave a surprise test in March on work covered in October? Everyone knows what would happen; that's why they don't do it. [7]

The contractual nature of the testing game—which students play by cramming, and teachers play by "being fair" and letting students know how to prepare for examinations—is evidence to me that most people who play the game know that it doesn't really work. That is, it doesn't work for people: it works fine for the educational system; testing is the best way to process students. But it does not help learning, and probably impedes it.

Gestalt theory describes this in terms analogous to eating: ideally, the organism approaches information like food—first experiencing hunger, then selecting what it needs, chewing it carefully, digesting it, making it a part of the whole self, and rejecting that which is not needed. If there is a kind of force-feeding and swallowing whole, there are a number of undesirable consequences—the organism will not develop in a natural and healthy way, it will probably develop an aversion to whatever has been forced upon it, and it will of course not assimilate much of what it has taken in. Mostly what we do in the process of being educated is gorge ourselves and throw up, sometimes the same material over and over again until we make it to that ultimate intellectual vomitorium, the doctoral examinations.

5. *Learning has no natural relationship to boredom; it does have a natural relationship to joy.* The reason boredom is so often experienced in educational situations is that so much of education is forced upon the student. I will turn again to gestalt theory, in which the person trying to force concentration is seen as experiencing a three-way division of energy: some energy is expended upon whatever is being studied, some flows toward more interesting "distractions," and some is used in fighting the interest in the distraction. There is plenty of excitement in such a situation, but it is not productive:

When one forces oneself to attend to what does not of itself draw one's interest, excitement accumulates, not toward this "chosen" object of attention, but in the struggle over the "distraction" which might really fire one's interest. . . . Meantime, as more and more of the excitement of attentiveness becomes committed to suppressing the disturber, what one is deliberately concentrating on is correspondingly more and more drained of interest. In short, it is boring.

Boredom occurs, then, when attention is deliberately paid to something lacking interest. The situation that *could* become interesting is effectively blocked. The result is fatigue and, eventually, trance. Suddenly attention switches from the boring situation to daydreaming.[8]

Boredom does not have to do with learning itself, but with an attempt to force into the organism something it does not want or need. If learning takes place under the right conditions, at the right time, it is a joyous experience; education can be, as George Leonard puts it, ecstasy.

John Holt's books, especially *How Children Learn*, contain a number of accounts of what goes on when people, young and old, spontaneously deal with material they want to learn and understand. One of the things that comes through powerfully in these stories is the exhilarating sense of achievement that accompanies understanding; another is the tremendous powers of concentration people have when they are dealing with things they want to figure out. The evidence clearly refutes the clichés about the limited "attention span" of small children; on the contrary, they are capable of just the kind of absorption in a problem and tenacity in staying with it until it is solved that we associate with the "disciplined" concentration of adults.

The Humanistic University

Those are, in a rather roughly summarized form, some of the key points of humanistic education. What we must now consider is how these concepts might be translated into working precepts in higher education. I am going to state a few general guidelines which seem to me to flow naturally from the humanistic perspective. These will be fairly unspecific: I suspect that, as this perspective begins to exert a greater influence in colleges and universities, many different forms will evolve from it. It is, after all, not so much an educational theory as an idea of what people are like. John Holt conveys the sense of this theory in the closing passage of *How Children Learn*:

In my mind's ear I can hear the anxious voices of a hundred teachers asking me, "How can you tell, how can you be sure what the children are learning, or even that they are learning anything?" The answer is simple. We can't tell. We can't be sure. What I am trying to say about education rests on a belief that, though there is much evidence to support it, I cannot prove, and may never be proved. Call it a faith. This faith is that man is by nature a learning animal. Birds fly, fish swim; man thinks and learns. Therefore, we do not need to "motivate" children into learning, by wheedling, bribing, or bullying. We do not need to keep picking away at their minds to make sure they are learning. What we need to do, and all we need to do, is bring as much of the world as we can into the school and the classroom; give children as much help and guidance as they need and ask for; listen respectfully when they feel like talking; and then get out of the way. We can trust them to do the rest.[9]

Holt is talking about educating children, but I think his idea of what we need to do is equally applicable to the education of adults in colleges and universities. In fact I am going to borrow one of his recommendations as Point One of my own list of suggestions:

1. *Bring as much of the world as possible into the school and the classroom.* This means (1) bringing as much as possible of the students' world into the classroom, and (2) giving students every kind of exposure to other people and other life styles. Education in politics should be a continuous feast of encounters with people of every shade of political conviction, with officeholders and bureaucrats and politicians of all descriptions; with people who control politics and with people who are controlled by it. Whenever possible the classroom should be extended beyond the campus out into the world—into the fields, the offices, the factories, the hospitals, the prisons, the streets, the mountains and deserts.

I would also like to see a much greater integration of adult education and "lifelong learning" programs with regular higher education, more mixture of the generations on the campuses, and many more opportunities for people to function simultaneously (or indistinguishably) as students and teachers.

2. *Give students control over their own education.* By control I mean considerably more than the opportunity to choose a major or a sequence of courses; I mean real participation in deciding what education is to be. There are already institutions, and special programs within institutions, which allow students to map out entire educational programs and even hire their own faculty. These are a promising model.

Educators who come into contact with such programs are often disturbed by the open expression of personal feelings and by the confusion, frustration, and uncertainty which are so evident, especially in the early stages of work—what encounter-group leaders call the "milling-around" phase. These things are, however, an important and valuable part of the educational process itself. Confusion, frustration and uncertainty are confronted in life—at least whenever one takes responsibility for it and does not submit to being a cipher in a programmed world—and our overorganized educational systems provide disastrously poor training for life planning.

Structure does, by the way, emerge from groups—such as groups of students—when they are given the opportunity to create it. I have been a part of organizations which have literally created themselves, from the people up, through the encounter-group process, and I know how satisfying and meaningful this form-making experience can be.

Rogers and others have explored the idea of the encounter group, rather than the classroom, as the basic educational unit; Rogers also suggests that the role of the teacher be changed to that of a "facilitator of learning." This role would require not so much knowledge of a given subject as skills of stimulating group interaction and self-discovery. Foremost among these skills, according to Jack and Lorraine Gibb, is the ability to create a climate of trust:

> Trust is the pacemaker variable in group growth. From it stem all the other significant variables of health. That is, to the extent that trust develops, people are able to communicate genuine feelings and perceptions on relevant issues to

all members of the system. To the degree that trust is present, people are able to communicate with themselves and others to form consensual goals. To the degree that trust is present, people can be truly interdependent.[10]

Apropos of this, it should be noted that controlling one's own education also means self-evaluation. It should be understood, however —and this is a point that people who leap too quickly into humanistic education sometimes miss—that self-evaluation does not take place in a vacuum. The function of some of the policies I have already suggested—maximum exposure to people and life-situations, the encounter-group educational structure—is not only to provide stimulation and guidance but also to provide the student with a maximum of opportunities for meaningful self-evaluation in doing things, observing other people doing things, and receiving open and honest feedback.

3. *Recognize that education is growth.* We need to develop, to a much greater degree than has been done thus far, a sensitivity toward what happens to people who are going through a learning process—what individuals need, how they take in different things at different times, what conditions nourish learning and change, what crises are experienced. This approach means that educators and administrators and students—everybody who participates in anything called a learning process—must be concerned with *all* of what learning is, and not only with the fragment of it which we now take to be the total phenomenon of education. We should be talking about growth and change, and developing our awareness of what human growth and change are.

It does not follow from this reasoning that educators must take over direction of more and more aspects of students' lives. It is quite possible to increase concern and simultaneously reduce control; that is a basic part of the humanistic approach to therapy, and it applies equally to education. The task is to provide opportunities and stimulation, make guidance and communication available and then, as John Holt says, get out of the way.

This guideline does not mean that the educator or administrator in a humanistic institution plays a merely passive role. On the contrary, there is plenty to do; the work just has a different focus. Douglas McGregor offered some insights into this some years ago in his paper on alternative theories of administration: his "Theory X," which embodies most of the current implicit assumptions we have already discussed, is a behavior-control approach:

The educational administrator who follows the usual pattern in carrying responsibility for his school sees his task as that of harnessing the energy of faculty and students so that the goals and requirements of the educational system will be met. In the first place he sees himself as responsible for organizing the available money, equipment, and people in such a way as to achieve the educational goal which he has in view. This means that he must motivate and direct his faculty, and through them the students. It means that one of his main functions is to control the actions and to modify the behavior of all members of the school in such ways that the educational goal would be achieved. Central to his policies is the view that both faculty and students would be, if left to their own devices, apathetic to, or resistant to, the educational goal. Consequently, they must be rewarded, punished, persuaded—through the use of both the carrot and the stick—so that they work toward the goal which the administrator, or his board of trustees, or the state, has defined as "being educated."

This usual approach to educational administration has implicit in it a rather definite view of the nature of the human being. It is implied that both teacher and student are naturally apathetic and tend to avoid any strenuous effort. Both teacher and student are seen as disliking responsibility and preferring to be guided or led.[11]

The other approach, which McGregor called "Theory Y," sees the administrator as another kind of facilitator of education and growth:

In terms of this theory the educational administration is responsible for organizing the resources of the institution—the teachers, the students, the funds, the equipment and materials in such a way that all of the persons involved can work together toward defining and achieving *their own* educational goals. The mainspring of the organization is the motivation for development and learning which is inherent in each person. The task of the administrator is to so arrange the organizational conditions and methods of operation so that people can best achieve their own goals by also furthering the jointly defined goals of the institution. The administrator finds that his work consists primarily of removing obstacles such as "red tape," of creating opportunities where teachers and students and administrators (including himself) can freely use their potential, of encouraging growth and change, and of creating a climate in which each person can *believe* that his potential is valued, his capacity for responsibility is trusted, his creative abilities prized.[12]

Part of the administrator's function in relation to the wider conception of human learning which I have discussed would be to decompartmental-ize educational experiences—to facilitate affective development as well as cognitive development, and to enable individuals to organize the different learning experiences into patterns of personal growth. Some college communities do provide a wealth of opportunities for personal change and development; I say college communities, because the colleges themselves are usually concerned only with cognitive education. Most of the social life, political involvements, communal living, efforts at personal growth in encounter groups, Yoga, meditation and so forth, are "off-campus," frequently discouraged and distrusted by administrators, and only rarely and haphazardly integrated into what goes on in the classroom. I am suggesting that every effort should be made to help students put the parts together, to integrate living with learning.

Brown's "confluent education" approach addresses itself to the task of helping the individual to grow as a whole person by developing the affective domain and the cognitive domain simultaneously and harmoni-ously. A large part of this work has to do with helping the individual to become more aware of his or her own needs and feelings and ways of relating to the environment; this process involves a number of experien-tial techniques, largely derived from gestalt awareness training, and it has to do with my fourth basic guideline for humanistic higher education.

4. *Orient education toward life-experience rather than toward subjects.* All education, of course, is derived from human experience—somebody's, but not the student's. The things that are taught are what Moreno calls cultural conserves; the data is retained, canned, and passed on, but the total human activity of which it was once a part cannot be so easily transmitted. Brown puts it this way:

> Most of the content of the curriculum in our classrooms originally had its source in human experience. When that live experience was transmuted into what was hoped would be a more efficient ordering of the curriculum, its vitality was usually lost. The educator, when justifying the transmutation, would argue, for example, that it was not possible for each student to learn the history of mankind by re-experiencing all the events on which it was based, or, for another example, that there was not time for the student himself to complete the sequence of mathematical frustrations followed by the excitement of insight that successive mathematicians throughout time had experienced, which gave mathematics a body of knowledge.
>
> Instead, educators, by compressing and organizing knowledge in all areas of the curriculum, have created in the classroom what Paul Tillich has called the fatal pedagogical error—''To throw answers like stones at the heads of those who have not yet asked the questions.''[13]

To get away from this is fairly simple, and has to do, again, with trusting the human desire to learn and recognizing the growth process in which every individual is involved. You begin by considering the possibility that the personal preoccupations of students—the drives, needs, hangups, ambitions, living experiments, idealistic commitments, all the things which are so widely dismissed as obstructions and distractions—are natural focal points for education: not merely subjects of interest, but potential guidelines for organizing educational programs which would be as useful and sensible as any of the present disciplines.

We are all so beguiled by the neatness and apparent logic of the division of knowledge into separate academic disciplines; it is quite difficult to remember that every student comes into the educational institution in possession of something that quite easily unites and transcends them all—that is, a human life. We lose sight of this fact—so do students, of course, in a lifetime of fragmentation—but it is there waiting to be appreciated and used. Every one of us has deep feelings and concerns which are, among other things, biological, historical, psychological, economic, political, social, and philosophical. To find some principle for ordering these ''subjects,'' one need look no further than one's own skin.

It will do a great deal to improve higher education if we can begin to lessen our dependence on the separately organized disciplines. They convey the impression of representing right and enduring ways of ordering the search for knowledge, but they do not; what they do is put blinkers on students and faculty alike and—especially at the graduate level—make the educational process mainly one of being intensely socialized into a small and cliquish academic world. The value of the present system of disciplines is professional and administrative, not educational. It has not been around as long as its present solidity would indicate, and I personally hope it will not be around too much longer.[14]

I am sure that many people who are now teaching the social sciences will feel, as they read these pages, the threat of being abandoned by change. What would be the place of the person who has ground his or her way through the old educational mill, in all this free learning?

Right in the middle of it, is my opinion. New universities are not going to spring full blown from our ideas of how things ought to be; they are going to grow out of our experience of how things are, and I think that one of the most important sources of ideas for shaping new educational models will be those who have functioned under the old. The principle of orienting education toward life experience applies to teachers and administrators as well as students, to the old and the square as well as the young and the hip, and to the forms of education itself. We will shape the future by looking hard at our thoughts and feelings about the present—by considering the possibility that the boredom and anger and nameless dissatisfaction we all experience in teaching and learning are not things to be shoved aside, but important clues to what we need and what education might possibly be. It is not the path which is the difficulty, Kierkegaard said; rather, it is the difficulty which is the path.

Notes

[1]George B. Leonard, *Education and Ecstasy* (New York: Delacorte Press, 1968) p. 124.

[2]Rogers, *Freedom to Learn* (Columbus, Ohio: Merrill, 1969), pp. 170–183.

[3]See Eulau quote, p. 79.

[4]*Freedom to Learn*, p. 158.

[5]George Brown, *Human Teaching for Human Learning: An Introduction to Confluent Education* (New York: Viking, 1971), p. 11.

[6]*Freedom to Learn*, p. 158.

[7]Holt, John, *How Children Fail* (New York: Pitman Publishing Corporation, 1964) p. 135. Reprinted by permission of the publisher.

[8]*Gestalt Therapy*, pp. 55–56.

[9]Holt, *How Children Learn* (New York: Pitman, 1967), p. 189.

[10]Jack R. and Lorraine M. Gibb, "Humanistic Elements in Group Growth," in *Challenges of Humanistic Psychology* (see ch. 1, fn. 16), pp. 162–3.

[11]*Freedom to Learn*, p. 206, summarizing McGregor, D. M., "The Human Side of Enterprise," in *The Planning of Change*, eds. W. G. Bennis, K. D. Benne and R. Chin (New York: Holt, Rinehart and Winston, 1961), pp. 431–442.

[12]*Ibid.*, p. 208.

[13]Brown, *Human Teaching*, pp. 15–16.

[14]This issue is discussed at greater length in my essay, "Beyond Disciplines," in Glass and Staude, *Humanistic Society*. See also Christopher Jencks and David Riesman, *The Academic Revolution* (New York: Doubleday, 1968); and Theodore Roszak, ed., *The Dissenting Academy* (New York: Random House, 1967).

XIII. Politics As Growth

I am convinced that our profession will never help us to advance from our wasteful, cruel, pluralist pseudopolitics in the direction of justice and humane politics until we replace political systems *with concepts of* human need *and* human development *as the ultimate value framework for our political analysis.*

—Christian Bay[1]

Change is one of the central things that humanistic psychology is about. Change and growth are taken to be the essential processes of human life, and obstacles to change are dealt with as chief sources of human misery. Gestalt, for example, regards blocking of awareness as one human strategy for resisting growth, and gestalt therapists regard themselves as facilitators of personal growth. The main thrust of research and theorizing in humanistic psychology is toward a comprehensive understanding of how human beings develop and grow.

Now, it is undoubtedly true that so far the emphasis in humanistic psychology has been upon individual, personal growth. When humanistic psychologists have addressed themselves to the possibility of bringing about widespread *social* change they have often tended to emphasize the incremental results of individual growth—such as the cumulative effect of many people undergoing some kind of personal transformation through therapy or encounter-group experience. There has been less of an inclination to consider the possible ways of changing institutions, or to understand institutional change as a way of facilitating personal growth for great numbers of people. Although I am reluctant to make too much of disciplinary distinctions, it might clarify the matter to say that we have developed a humanistic psychology, but are only at the beginning of thinking about a humanistic political science and a humanistic polity.

Yet humanistic psychology does offer guidelines for looking at institutions—and changing and creating them—in terms of human needs and human development. Maslow's hierarchy of needs, Hampden-Turner's model of psychosocial development, both address themselves directly to the question of how social arrangements can facilitate, or obstruct, the growth of human beings. They offer propositions which are testable according to the empirical standards of contemporary social science research, and they lead rather easily to ideas about public policy. It requires no great interdisciplinary stretch of the mind to see the political implications of Maslow's need-hierarchy theory, to see where beneath issues of public policy are issues of human development. For example:

Poverty—when people are deprived of the fundamental necessities, as are millions of Americans and even more millions of human beings in other countries, their capacity for development is frustrated at the most basic level.

Sex—taken to be another one of the fundamental physiological needs, and yet sexual frustration is one of the most prevalent features of life in most cultures, so common that its presence is taken for granted as a natural condition of civilized existence. And the great majority of governmental actions in this area—state laws, police procedures, educational policies, etc.—are in support of sexual repression.

Work—greatly valued in our society, but we place far too much emphasis on the physical productivity of work and far too little on the experience of work as a satisfaction of the needs of individuals who perform it. Good working experiences can contribute toward the satisfaction of a number of needs—safety, belongingness, esteem, self-actualization in the truest and highest sense—but working experiences in which the needs of human beings are denied (and I fear this means the vast majority of modern jobs, both high and low paying) thwart the developmental potential of the individuals who perform them.

In one way or another, the above issues touch the lives of all of us. This is important to bear in mind, because we must deal with the question of whether a humanistic, developmental perspective in politics has a universal relevance.

Humanistic psychology, and the broader human potential movement of which it is a part, are sometimes characterized as upper-middle-class affairs, relevant only to the needs and interests of well-educated white Americans. There is just enough truth in this statement to make the matter worth considering, because by doing so we can come to a clearer understanding of what a humanistic orientation to politics really means, or can mean.

It is undoubtedly true that the encounter-group movement, which is the most visible part of humanistic psychology in contemporary society, is mainly an activity of upper-middle-class whites. It is not exclusively that, because of various community organizations, interracial groups, consciousness-raising groups, public agencies, and private organizations such as Synanon. But the cost of group therapy, and of the programs at the various growth centers, is high enough to select out a large segment of the population. And those group programs (such as sensitivity training) which are instituted with the blessing of management in private industry are usually for the benefit of executives, not workers.

It is also true that self-actualization theory rests mainly on a basis of research with white intellectuals. The historical figures studied in Maslow's original research were, with only a few exceptions, white males, and the young people studied for signs of development toward self-actualization were all college students.[2]

Yet the encounter-group movement is not all of humanistic psychology—encounter addresses itself to a specific range of needs, not to all needs—and I believe that the drive toward self-actualization is, as Maslow insisted, species-wide and not peculiar to any race, culture, or sex. The predominance of white males among the historical figures considered to be examples of self-actualized people is not so much a flaw in Maslow's research as evidence of the inadequacy of a society which offers such a narrow spectrum of its members the opportunity to reach their fullest development as human beings.

I would argue, then, that the middle-class bias is relatively superficial, and that humanistic psychology is in fact a comprehensive set of ideas relevant to the needs of *all* people. And it states quite clearly—more clearly, I think than most alternative ideologies or philosophies—that human needs, although capable of being ordered in a single conceptual framework, vary enormously from person to person and group to group according to time and environmental conditions. No informed student of humanistic psychology could argue that sensitivity training and meditation are the solution to poverty and racial inequality. Instead, humanistic psychology offers some specific propositions about the full range of human needs: what is likely to happen when they are not met and what is likely to happen when they *are* met.

Maslow's need-hierarchy theory, for example, tells us that when people are deprived of the basic life necessities they cannot normally be expected to mobilize themselves effectively toward the satisfaction of more complex social needs. This fact, as we have seen, is supported by research on deprivation, and it adds up to further support for guaranteed-annual-income programs which would help to remove the most fundamental obstacles to growth. Maslow's theory further states that when basic physiological needs *are* met, people will then turn their attention toward such "higher" needs as safety, belongingness, and esteem. But here again, development can be blocked; public policies which can and do block development at this level are welfare arrangements administered so as to keep recipients aware of the precariousness of their existence, which force them into a denigrated social status as the price of bare economic security.

Hampden-Turner's work, showing how individuals pass through various stages of psychosocial development—a passage which, again, can be either facilitated or blocked—gives us further insight into the human value of institutions. Like Maslow's need theory, Hampden-Turner's theory of psychosocial development urges us to look at institutions not merely in terms of how they function in the political system, but in terms of how they nourish or starve the people who participate in their activities.

These theories can generate some specific policy recommendations, but they do more than that: they also lead toward a different idea of what politics *is*. To get at what I mean let me cite a few general statements about politics by leading political scientists. Robert Dahl: "A political system is any persistent pattern of human relationships that involves, to a significant extent, power, rule, or authority."[3] Heinz Eulau: "I suggest that what makes man's behavior political is that he rules and obeys, persuades and compromises, promises and bargains, coerces and represents, fights and fears. . . ."[4] And of course Harold Lasswell's oft-quoted definition of politics as a matter of "who gets what, when, and how."[5]

These definitions all tell us something about politics, and they also tell us something about the range of vision of the definers, what it is that they have chosen to see. They show us the established paradigm, the framework within which political phenomena are perceived as such and subjected to analysis.

But suppose we define politics as the ways people organize themselves in order to attain the greatest satisfaction of human needs possible within the environment.

This definition is quite compatible with those above; it merely serves to call our attention to certain matters which contemporary political science neglects. It allows us, for one thing, to see politics as part of a biological process, as discussed in chapter 8; and it encourages us to look at politics not merely as a system, or patterns of action, but as an enterprise guided by a purpose.

Christian Bay, one of the very few political scientists who has shown an awareness of the political dimensions of Maslow's work, argues that the bias against value-laden or normative concepts in modern social science has led to a preoccupation with observable and measurable demands only, to the kind of behavior that he calls "pseudopolitics."[6] The trouble with this emphasis upon demands is that it turns our attention toward those who do the demanding—which usually means organized interest groups—and relieves us of the necessity of considering the possibility that there may be many people within the political order who have needs which are never effectively stated or heard as political demands. It also diverts political analysis from a critical evaluation of whether the system's demand-satisfactions are in fact need-satisfactions—whether the public policies, the goods and services provided by the working of the economy, really effectively satisfy the needs, facilitate the optimum development and growth, of human beings.

The way of looking at politics which I am advocating here certainly does not require us to believe that all political orders perform the job of satisfying human needs equitably or efficiently. It is quite obvious that for the great majority of human beings alive today even the most fundamental needs—food, shelter, etc.—are not being satisfied, and it is also probably true that even in the most wisely ordered societies the general level of development of individual members is far below their potential. I say "probably," because the social sciences, so far, have not acquired that kind of knowledge.

When we look at politics this way we naturally turn our attention to the things that obstruct human development. And I believe that the most important single limiting factor is the idea which any society has about what the possibilities of human development actually are. A stunted or narrow conception of the human potential, especially when deeply built into cultural norms and reinforced by a society's art and science and philosophy, is as powerful a form of tyranny as any political institution. By stunted or narrow conception I mean any lopsided view which focuses on certain human needs—safety or esteem, for example—to the exclusion of others, or a truncated value system such as our own which sees the acquisition of a great amount of material goods and social prestige as evidence of the upper limits of human growth.

The historical importance of humanistic psychology is that it offers us a new and more expansive vision of human growth, at a time when the shortcomings of the old vision have become most evident.

And although I have argued that humanistic psychology has something to say about the full range of human needs, I must insist here that in order to understand its value as a new paradigm, a basically new way of thinking about humanity, we must not accept only its more respectable components. The humanistic perspective is altogether too easily trimmed at its outer edges and absorbed neatly into the existing paradigm. We have already seen that Maslow's theories, as interpreted by Davies, found their way rather painlessly into political science; the only thing that got lost along the way was the meaning of self-actualization.[7]

But humanistic psychology is relatively unimportant if we leave out its esoteric component. Unless we are prepared to deal seriously with self-actualization, with the development of consciousness, with the insights of Eastern philosophy, with meditation and the neo-Reichian physical therapies, with bio-feedback research and all it implies, then we cannot say that we have truly confronted the challenge of humanistic psychology. It challenges our commonly held beliefs about what people are, how they grow and change, and what they may become. Humanistic psychology is significant only insofar as it pushes and tugs at fundamental ideas.

It seems to me that if we are guided at all times by some kind of image of the upper reaches of human development, then our way of considering matters of public policy will be fundamentally different. We will not be trying—to use welfare again as a point of reference—to remove a potential source of crime or even to make certain individuals more "socially productive," but rather to release the fullest possibilities of human development. Guided by such a perspective, we are likely to create policies and institutional forms considerably different from those now being proposed by reformers—many of whom, like those in power, tend to think almost exclusively in terms of material goods and political coercion. Certainly we would create policies far different from the ones we now have. Our politics, like our psychology, has lost touch with a concept of human health. We think mainly in terms of acute social ailments and first-aid remedies, rarely in terms of the fullest possibilities of human growth and how societies may facilitate it.

I fear that our political science has supported this kind of thinking—

take a look again at the above definitions of politics. It has made the most outrageous symptoms of political sickness—the inequitable distribution of goods and services, the conflicts for power and special advantage, the manipulation of the public by officeholders and office seekers—seem like the norms of civilized life. This "realism" has conspired to banish the search for a more sane and nourishing social order to the realm of idealism, and thus deprive it of intellectual legitimacy.

But the search—because it, too, expresses a deep and very real human drive—goes on anyway. And in service of it we have available to us now a somewhat different conception of human life, which forms the unifying framework of humanistic psychology. It also forms the theoretical basis for the technology—rather, the many technologies—of humanistic therapy and encounter-group work. These technologies have touched the lives of thousands of people, and have undoubtedly accounted for some degree of social change. But their application is still fairly limited. We have not, nor has any society in history, made it an effort of high priority to understand the processes and possibilities of human growth and to translate that understanding into social policy. Yet the opportunity to do so is clearly being presented to us.

If we should choose to seize upon this opportunity, to make the highest development of human beings a deliberate social goal, then the task before us is to think about the growth possibilities of all people, at all social and economic levels, and also to understand fully what it means when a species begins to become responsible for its own evolution. As we consider such questions the humanistic perspective becomes not merely psychological, but political. We are not talking about principles of research or therapy, but about principles of social action and institutional change. Our new vision of the possibilities of human existence becomes a set of guidelines for building a human community; it is no longer the concern merely of writers and clinicians and social scientists but a *res publica*, a public thing.

Notes

[1]Christian Bay, "The Cheerful Science of Dismal Politics," in *The Dissenting Academy*, ed. Theodore Roszak (New York: Random House, Inc. and Pantheon Books, a Division of Random House, Inc. 1967), p. 232.

[2]*Motivation and Personality* (see ch. 4, fn. 3), pp. 150–152.

[3]Robert Dahl, *Modern Political Analysis* (Englewood Cliffs, N.J.: Prentice-Hall, 1963), p. 6.

[4]Eulau, *The Behavioral Persuasion in Politics*, pp. 4–5.

[5]Lasswell, *Politics: Who Gets What, When, How* (New York: Peter Smith, 1950).

[6]See Bay, "Cheerful Science," also "Politics and Pseudopolitics: A Critical Evaluation," in Charles A. McCoy and John Playford, *Apolitical Politics: A Critique of Behavioralism* (New York: Crowell, 1967).

[7]Knutson's book (see ch. 9, fn. 6) shows a much better grasp of the meaning of self-actualization. However, Davies' work is still accepted by most political scientists as the standard political application of Maslow's theories.

Index

Walt Anderson

Politics and the New Humanism

Can traditional politics respond to the affirmation goals of such human-istic psychologists as A. H. Maslow, Carl Rogers, and F. S. Perls?

This is one of the key questions that Walt Anderson asks as he strikes a new direction in political science and explores the political dimensions of humanistic psychology. In this book Anderson demonstrates that tra-ditional Freudian and behaviorist psychologies are forces of political conservatism in which personal needs are sacrificed to existing social conditions.

FEATURES

Discusses Abraham Maslow's search for a psychology based on health and human potential, rather than on mental illness, and the social-policy implications of Maslow's work.

Traces the origins of the encounter group movement in the United States and argues that this movement is not only a way of dealing with personal alienation, but a social and potentially political movement attempting to transform the basic values of our culture.

Critiques Freudian theory as having created a school of political analysis that sees political activism as evidence of personal neurosis.

Analyzes behaviorist psychology as being basically a technology of social control.

Outlines a theory of psycho-social development which interprets politi-cal behavior in terms of the psychological development of individuals rather than in terms of social class, group membership or economic self interest.

GOODYEAR PUBLISHING CO.   0-87620-661-5
Pacific Palisades, California   Cover design by Fred Hartson